TAKING TER

CH01403469

A Love Affair
With A
Small Catamaran

Mathew Wilson

Published by
PARADISE CAY PUBLICATIONS
Post Office Box 20
Middletown, CA 95461

FIRST EDITION

ISBN 0939837 242

LIBRARY OF CONGRESS CATALOG CARD NUMBER:
94-068066

COVER PHOTO BY JENNIFER BURDICK

BACK COVER PHOTO BY EDWARD WILSON

Published by
PARADISE CAY PUBLICATIONS
Post Office Box 20
Middletown, CA 95461

Telephone (707) 987-3971

PRINTED IN THE UNITED STATES OF AMERICA

Sea Rabbit
with love . . .

THE STORY OF THE FIRST VOYAGE

OF A CRUISING CATAMARAN

FROM ENGLAND, THROUGH THE FRENCH

CANALS AND THE MEDITERRANEAN,

ACROSS THE ATLANTIC AND THE

CARIBBEAN,

TO HER DESTINED HOME IN FLORIDA

TABLE OF CONTENTS

CHARTS AND MAP

TIME AND DISTANCE

<u>1990</u>

March 31 - May 8	Birdham Pool, Chichester, England, to Sète, France. 1,030.67 nm
May 10 - 19	Sète, France, to Santa Pola, Alicante, Spain. 495.61 nm
October 23 - November 13	Santa Pola to El Puerto de Santa Maria, Cádiz Bay. 507.8 nm

<u>1991</u>

January 18 - 25	Santa Maria, Cádiz Bay, Spain, to Mogan, Gran Canaria. 760.53 nm
February 6 - 13	Mogan to Porto Grande, São Vicente, Cape Verde Islands. 831.67 nm
February 17 - March 7	São Vicente, Cape Verde Islands, to Bridgetown, Barbados. 2,011 nm
March 11 - April 17	Barbados to Virgin Gorda, British Virgin Islands. 495.15 nm

<u>1992</u>

January 29 - February 29	Virgin Gorda, British Virgin Islands, to Nassau, Bahamas. 925.64 nm
March 5 - 18	Nassau, Bahamas, to Jupiter Inlet, Florida, USA. 209.15 nm
<u>Total Distance</u>	±7,267.22 nm (allowing for log calibration errors).

IN THE BEGINNING

This is a simple story, written for enjoyment alone, to encourage those who dream of setting out to sail the seas and oceans of the world.

This is the story of a dream realized. There is nothing remarkable about that. Such transmutation, wish fulfillment, call it what you like, occurs more commonly than might be supposed. Mine was a long held dream, fifteen years in the making, years during which I'd been suffering from recurrent attacks of sailing fever. I thought of the warm, clear waters of the Mediterranean, of the Florida Keys and the Bahamas, and the Caribbean. I thought about getting a boat with the long-legged ability to cross the Pacific, to reach the Marquesas, and sail on through Polynesia. It was pure escapism. It was compulsive delusion: a kind of paranoia. I was a lousy sailor, time and time again chronically seasick whenever I put out to sea. I had no practical nautical skills. All I could claim was to have read a large number of sailing books, all of which had totally unhinged me by keeping the dream alive.

To cement my destabilization I sailed whenever I had the opportunity, wherever my real life, my working life, had taken me. It was mostly unpleasant. The North Sea too early in the year; and the North Sea and the English Channel too late in the year. Hong Kong in all seasons, with fickle winds and the inescapable green pollution of the Pearl River estuary. One memorable singularly alcoholic long weekend cruising in New Zealand's Hauraki Gulf, which gave me a lasting respect for a breed of people who preferred port to orange juice for breakfast. Florida and the Bimini Islands, with the Gulf Stream in-between kicking up white horses as if wild stallions were lashing out somewhere down there in that chaos of midnight blue water. To accelerate my descent down this millrace of inevitability, I set about finding a boat. Not a temporary playboat. A serious boat, for serious sailing, not Sunday poddling in bays and inlets. I had a wife and two children, none of whom shared my dementia. "I don't mind sailing, Daddy, but what I don't like is all this ready-abouting" was the very positive judgement of our daughter, aged eight. I knew this dreamboat had to be comfortable, it had to be sea kindly, safe, and easy to handle, even single-handed, for the family were bound to vote with their feet and decline to share in any more nautical adventures. If there was any way in which I could entice them on board, I was convinced it would be a big plus in family eyes if the dreamboat didn't heel, and it would win even more points if you could sunbathe on deck, use the boat as a swim platform, and even run it gently in to a shelving beach, ground without fear, and let the tide run out and picnic. On the level.

We'd tried all these recreational activities in a variety of craft ranging from a Mirror dinghy to a Chinese junk, which I'd bought on impulse along the way to seduce the family with the excitement of sailing your own boat. Nothing seemed to work out too well. The junk trips, to my mind the epitome of romantic coastal dream-boating, caused deep family despair whenever a new expedition was announced and a stampede of voting with feet. The junk was sold. I didn't regret it, for she rolled like a pig, and by then I'd set my heart on buying a catamaran. Out of all my early surveys only one boat seemed right at the outset, a stout little centre cockpit cat with a turtle-back and two monstrous looking rudders hanging at the back. The Heavenly Twins, first built in Cornwall in the 1970s, had evolved year by year into what might be called the perfect small ocean cruising catamaran, and it had certainly won high praise from Jim Andews, one of the foremost cat experts of the day. But real life took over again, and all my ideas of sailing went on the backburner for ten years, with a noticeable improvement in family morale.

Then in 1988 a new version of the old Heavenly Twins, my original dreamboat, was produced and almost by accident I saw the first one in the water. That was it. Thunder. Lightning. Catalysis. The only cure for blue water dementia is action. It was time to get going before I became senile, or hesitation and sensible prudence took over. I booked myself on a schooner sailing out of Boston to learn celestial navigation, and placed an order for a Heavenly Twins 27, a catamaran with an LOA just over 26 feet, measuring 21ft 6ins on the waterline. It was not, you might say, a very large craft; but it was a very great step for me.

The boat that was to become *Terrapin*, named for her lines, that turtle-back, her agility, and her diminutive size, was ordered in May 1989 for delivery in March 1990. Moulding started in Plymouth, England, in June 1989 and the boat was to be launched in Falmouth in March 1990. I live in the United States and envisaged

Terrapin eventually based on the East Coast of Florida where I had already arranged a mooring. For nine months I questioned my sanity in building a boat in Cornwall, almost within sight of Land's End, while I was living on the other side of the Atlantic; and I questioned my wisdom in insisting that she be fitted wholly with US-bought electrics and electronics, which was migraine-inducing, if nothing else. Then, as the fitting problems slowly sorted themselves out, the realization dawned (had it always been dormant?) that there were only two ways in which *Terrapin* could reach her intended home in Florida. She could be shipped there as deck cargo; or she could make it on her own.

You start to make decisions and the line of thought runs on. You're in England, and you have a boat and you want to cross the Atlantic. It's got to be a trade wind passage, and it's got to be in the winter because the summer breeds hurricanes. You have to get south to start but Biscay is bad, treacherous all winter, and the western coastline of Europe is unwelcoming until the North Atlantic summer barometric Highs become stationary, long after the sun has crossed the Equator on its journey north. So in winter you must first get to Cádiz or Gibraltar, somewhere around there, for the best entry gate to the southern half of the North Atlantic, which is also, of course, the exit from the Mediterranean. Suddenly everything snaps into place. The canals of France are the dream route to the Mediterranean, are they not? It's not just seizing on them as the only alternative to the fear of a hellish offshore passage across the Bay of Biscay. It's not negative. It's the positive side of heading up the Seine. Images of April in Paris and mental color prints of the lazy waterways of the Loire. The anticipation of dining in remote country inns, the *petites auberges*, the *relais*, the small restaurants of the real France, for who would pass them by on a 'once-in-a-lifetime' trip; and why not taste burgundy in Burgundy, drink *Côtes du Rhône* on the Rhône, and see Avignon and the Camargue? And then take a few days in the South of France to make ready for sea; and head for winter sunshine in the Balearic Islands? Was there ever a choice?

Popularly catamarans are still regarded as suspect, unstable craft, potentially suicidal as they can overturn under stress and will never right themselves. It's true about the righting, which could spoil your day; but then again, if you want to dwell on worst case scenarios, just remind yourself that if a keelboat fills with water, it will surely sink. Now Alan Butler, a retired Canadian, had taken an early Heavenly Twins single-handed around the world in 1980-86, rumor had it that a Swiss-owned boat was, even then, half way through a circumnavigation; and someone said another HT had won the multihull class in the first ARC (the annual Atlantic Rally for Cruisers). It seemed encouraging. The boat might make it, if she could squeeze through the locks of the French canals; but could I make it? I felt about as ready as I would have felt at the age of six if I'd been asked to ride my new tricycle in the Tour de France. Negative thinking can keep you in your armchair or paralyzed with anticipatory fright as you lie wide awake, flat on your back in your bed at night. Just make the plan and get going. Launch the boat in March. Take it to the Mediterranean through the French

Canals. Get to Gibraltar and hole up there for the summer. Come back in the winter and get to the Canaries. Cross to Barbados. Then go lotus-eating up the island chain to the Bahamas and be in Florida well before August, for that's the start of the hurricane season. Obvious? That's almost the way it was; but it wasn't this way at all. For, despite all my schooling, I knew nothing when I set out.

Just before *Terrapin* was launched, Janet and I were in Karachi staying with friends to attend a series of New Year weddings. Between the mega receptions and parties we killed time wandering around the bazaars, and there, in a shop selling nothing but Baluchistan onyx carvings, I found a tiny terrapin for sale, barely an inch and a half long. Later, mounted in a frame of Vermont cherry, the little terrapin become the lodestar of her boat. As it was, the night we bought the little onyx terrapin we were caught up in what we thought was a massive New Year's celebration. Janet was impressed by the fireworks, which we could hear exploding in ragged patterns all around us but at street level, crushed in a jam of overexcited people and gridlocked traffic, we couldn't see the bursts in the sky.

There were no starbursts. It was rifle fire. I think we were lucky to get away.

"It'll be better at sea" I said as we caught our breath, still hoping to sign her on as Mate.

Promises. Promises.

I'm not certain I was right. Oh, the business of taking *Terrapin* home was all that I'd promised. It was good. But there were times when, had I seen the future in my crystal ball, I might have paused to reflect on the absolute necessity of my voyaging. But Janet should have said 'yes' in Karachi, and I can't think why she didn't rush to sign on. Is there a lesson in it? Yes. Attend to your crew recruitment, right at the start. Don't leave it until too late. People get distracted when the shooting starts.

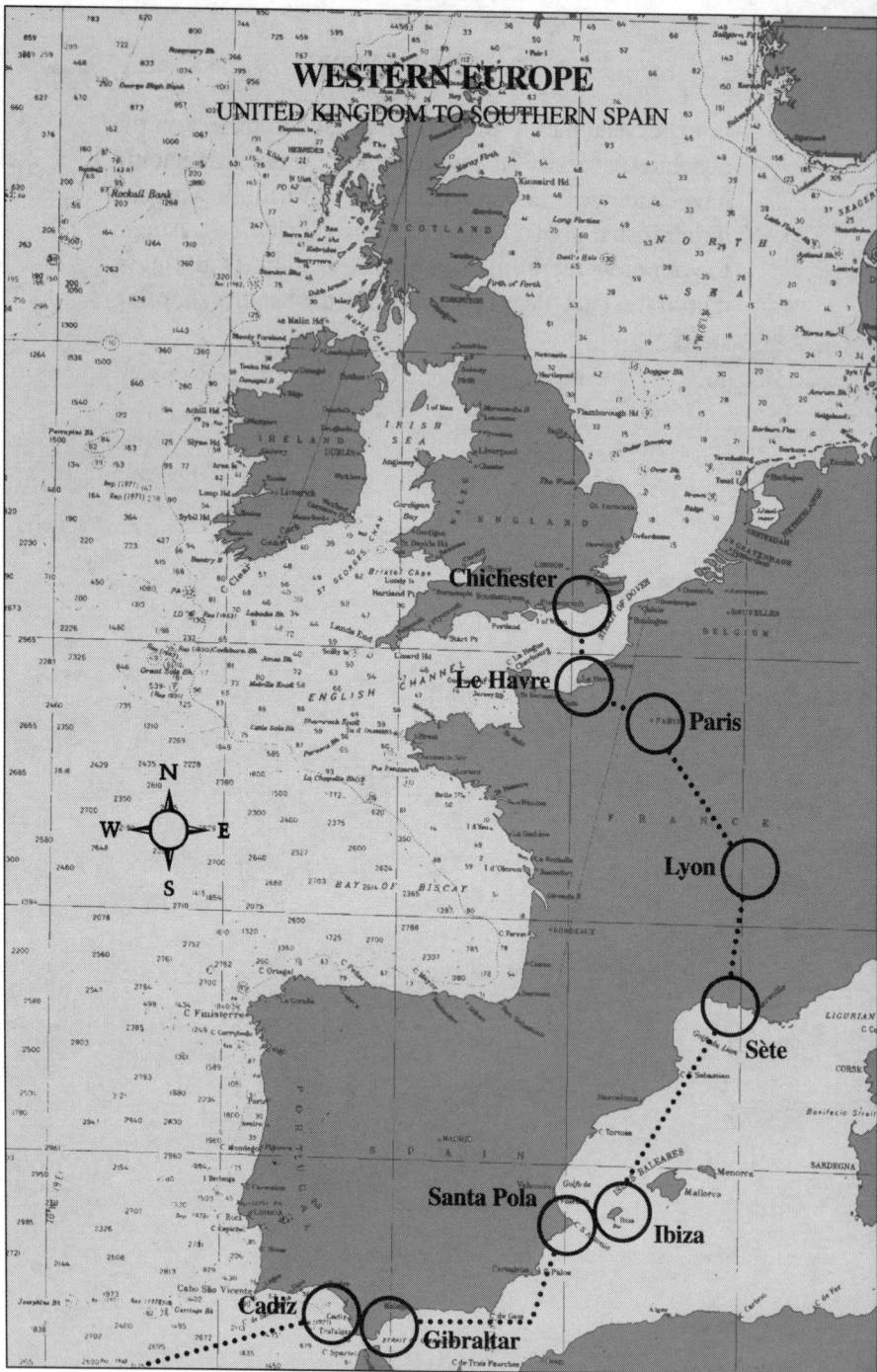

WESTERN EUROPE
UNITED KINGDOM TO SOUTHERN SPAIN

THE FIELDS OF FRANCE

Birdham Pool, Chichester, England, to Sète, France.
March 31 - May 8 1990

By the end of March 1990 *Terrapin* had been
delivered from the builders and was at Birdham, near
Chichester, on the south coast of England. It was bitterly
cold, freezing each night, and I was living on board, fed
up to the back teeth and ready to call the whole thing off.
Three days before my target departure date *Terrapin* had
yet to be fitted with her sprayhood and bimini, her twin
Yanmar 1GM10 9 hp diesels were still due their initial
service, the compass had not been swung, none of the
Autohelm ST-50 sailing instruments were calibrated,
and both the main and the staysail had gone back to North
Sails for modifications. I was living in chaos, nothing
had found a permanent home in the constant upheaval,
and the boatyard showers were a nightmare.

The chance of spending two days on sea trials had
gone straight out of the window. Birdham Pool is tide
dependent, you are either locked-in or locked-out for
much of the day, and the sailmakers and the mechanics
insisted that they needed the boat at hand, so that was it.
No shake down. A night Channel crossing would be
Terrapin's commissioning, which was a little like elect-
ing to jump into the deep end of a pool before you had
learned to swim. In truth I needed the shore time. I had
yet to provision the boat and *Terrapin* needed to be fitted
with what I was told was vital protection against the perils

of the French locks to come: at least five car tires slung each side in addition to her normal fenders, with extra long fender boards made ready to be used in all the horror places, where the lock walls or canal embankments were corrugated steel plate or nothing but rusty pilings. The dire warnings about the hazards of the French canal system and the urgency of advice from canal veterans was endless. So I went to the local tire kingdom to scavenge old tires and the timber yard to buy massive planks of rough cut timber. Industrial plastic sheeting had to be cut and rigged ready to be hung as aprons under the tires to prevent black scoring on her virgin white hull, and outfitting *Terrapin* with her new unsightly dress, and then stowing it all away, seemed to take forever. Finally extra warps were needed. The minimum, so my prophets of doom told me, was a 10 meter line fore and aft each side and two 20 meter lines for the deep locks. And the list went on. You have crutches for the mast and boom, ready for when the mast has to be taken down? Oh, and you'll need two boat hooks, not just one, ready for your crew to pole-off the locksides; and oh yes, you'll need two mooring spikes, at least two foot long, with a sledgehammer to drive them in. You aren't allowed to moor on the canals using trees, and in many places there's nothing but grass bank anyway . . . And somehow I completed the largest supermarket buying trip I have ever made and nearly went into cardiac arrest when the total was rung up on the cash register.

My morale seemed to be plummeting rather than surging with excitement. All I wanted to do was check into a good hotel and forget the whole venture. Then

Martyn Medcalf, *Terrapin*'s builder, joined me for the first leg to Paris. It was Saturday March 31st and the weather didn't look good: wind becoming easterly rising to Force 6 within 24 hours. If we delayed, we'd have to sit it out. As it was, we might have it on the nose all the way. If there's one thing that catamarans like even less than keel boats, it's fighting headwinds for it's inefficient, the bridgedeck slams, it's uncomfortable, fatiguing, and noisy. But there are times when, unless it's outright foolish to move, journeys must start.

We set out that afternoon, roughly calibrated the instruments after passing over Chichester Bar, and headed straight for Le Havre. Twenty hours and 102 miles later, with more motorsailing than I cared for, we were there. It had been a black, cold, wet, and bumpy night with short seas, increasing wind shifting to the east, right on the nose, the smart new yellow sprayhood blew in, and we slammed our way across enough shipping lanes, conveyor belts of red, green, and white lights and vast ill-defined silhouettes, to sustain anxiety at peak level. We took turn and turn about, dividing the night into two hour watches. It was long enough in the cockpit under those conditions. From the outset we used GPS to navigate for there was no sun, no planets and stars, and no land; and then there were no satellites after 2100 until 0247 the next day, for the GPS satellite deployment program was far from complete. So it was DR for six hours. Somehow we made it right on track to the Le Havre entry channel and motored in to the yacht harbor in sudden, surprising sunshine which had us out of foul weather gear and straight into tee-shirts. By the time we'd had showers at the local Yacht Club, the horrors of the night were forgotten.

We folded the Channel chart and opened the first of our library of river and canal guides to take our first serious look at the Seine. It's 80 miles up river from Le Havre to Rouen (I'm talking nautical miles now) and that is as far as an ocean going ship can get. It's the point at which your mast must be taken down, for there are no opening bridges on the rivers and canals of France. I suppose we could have taken the mast down at Le Havre, but decided, just for fun, to sail as far as we could. The next day, as if in compensation for the lousy weather of the Channel crossing, we entered the Seine with the tide and the wind just right. In one splendid run with the wind gusting Force 3 - 5 we went tearing past Honfleur and shot under the great arc of the Pont de Tancarville, Europe's longest suspension bridge, at seven and a half knots; but the sailing ended all too soon and the engine hours were clicking up long before we reached Rouen at 2000 that evening. The following morning we declared ourselves to the port authorities, and 250 francs ($45) secured ten minutes help from a local crane operator as we unstepped the mast. The charge seemed extortionate. It was, we were assured, the market price. There were no options. It was time then to shake out the plastic skirts, get out the tires and the boards, and complete *Terrapin*'s involuntary and temporary change of role from sailing craft to canal boat.

It took us three days to cover the 193 miles from Rouen to Paris, putting in overlong twelve hour days at the helm. The Seine is one of the commercial arteries of northern France and there are seven locks between Le Bas des Poses, some 50 miles upstream from Rouen, and Suresnes, in the outskirts of Paris itself. You cut your milk teeth learning canal skills given that kind of practice. You soon learn to keep clear of the front gates in ascending locks, for when the flood gates are opened the incoming water boils and the swell can hit you like a tidal bore. But the barges have priority in a lock, they enter first. Tucked in at the back, you generally have a gentle ride. All you have to do is hang on, watch your lines, and beware of the prop wash when everyone else takes off. *Terrapin* seemed like a cockleshell beside the double and triple barges and the football-field sized 'pusher' car carriers, but these monstrous craft are handled with a consummate skill that made us look, at times, as if we were steering with our feet. There's something unnerving, at the start, about the big locks which are remotely controlled by an unseen lock-keeper high in an airport-type control tower, but the system is slick, efficient, and there's no fooling around: you're in, out, and on your way, for it's a highway. No-one lingers.

No-one would expect a commercial waterway to be a garden route, but I thought the Seine upriver of Rouen might be more attractive than the lower reaches, which were a desolation. I was wrong. The river is a dumping ground for every town along its course and you can tell that it's bad: there's little riverbank wildlife, no waterfowl, nothing living there, and the water swirls covered in scum beneath the barrages by the locks. They run luxury river cruises through Upper Normandy now, but as a scenic stretch I think it would be low on my list.

There's Monet's Giverny, yes, but you don't need a boat to get there. Perhaps the best place was Les Andelys early in the morning with the mist still rising and the ruins of Château Gaillard, the castle Richard the Lionheart built in 1196, standing high on the white cliffs above the small town. That was magic.

It was dramatic entering Paris. The serpentine twisting of the river as you approach the capital gave the Seine its name, 'the Snake', and suddenly, after seeing just about every heading displayed on the compass card as we followed the bends through unending miles of grey industrial wasteland and tenement development, we were there. It was almost as if a stage curtain had been raised in front of us. There was no gradual change, no acclimatization. Lulled by the monotony of the approaches we were caught by surprise, rounded the 'last' bend and that was it. We were right in the heart of Paris, with the downstream tip of the Allée des Cygnes capped with its welcoming mini-copy of Bartholdi's Statue of Liberty right ahead and the Eiffel Tower to starboard. It would been good to take it slowly, but the pace of the river traffic forced us on, under the *belle époque* extravagance of the bridges one after another: Iena, Alma, Invalides, Alexandre III, and Concorde. It must be one of the most dramatic boat rides in the world. You wave at the people on the café roof terrace of the Musée d'Orsay and then suddenly you're passing the Ile de la Cité, Notre Dame is above you, immense, blocking the sky, and your branch of the river narrows to become an anxiety-inducing racetrack choked with *bateaux mouches* and barges. We turned to port off the Seine after passing the Ile St Louis, locking into the Canal St Martin to stay in the Port de Plaisance de Paris-Arsenal, between the Seine and the Place de la Bastille. It's the best mooring in Paris.

April in Paris should have been great but as ill-luck had it, Europe suffered a throwback to winter as a subzero air mass settled over northern France, and in comparison Birdham Pool seemed tropical. I cannot ever remember having been so paralyzed with cold, the kind of curl-up-in-a-tight-ball type cold, for we were long past shivering. The other half of the 'we' was Janet, who had just flown in from Boston. Martyn had gone off to build more boats. Friends from Northern Ireland, Edith and Victoria Gailey, mother and daughter, were holidaying in Paris and our daughter Victoria, with a week to go before her final exams at Cambridge, came for the weekend. She left, ashen-faced, flu well on its way, patently relieved to climb into the warmth of an airport bus. We set off with the Gaileys who wanted a river trip after enduring another day of arctic weather. Five minutes after we locked out of the Canal St Martin into the Seine, just as we were approaching the fuelling barge at the Pont d'Austerlitz, *Terrapin* gave a convulsive shudder and the port engine alarm screamed, startling the wits out of me. I shut it down. Shaft or propeller? The shaft looked OK when I inspected it after we were secure alongside the barge. Prop? Something wrapped around it? The Seine was too filthy to see anything. I had a mask and snorkel. Let the swimming ladder down and use them? Reluctant to strip, I asked the refuelling crew whether there was any chance of finding someone who would dive to check the prop, for I had none of my scuba gear on board then. It took a long time to get a suggestion: perhaps the Brigade Fluviale, the marine police, on the Quai Henri IV on the right bank, back towards Notre Dame, might help? We limped there on one engine. An hour later a police diver had freed the port propeller from the tangled shreds of a king-sized sheet of heavy plastic. Without a wet suit and scuba gear I could never have cleared it. Where had it come from? The Pont d'Austerlitz, just past the refuelling barge, was under repair wrapped in plastic sheeting. In my naiveté I'd thought that was one kind of accident I'd anticipated and prevented, for *Terrapin* has cutters fixed on both shafts. OK for fishing line, maybe, and plastic bags? But not anything else? How can you tell? They say you never know how well your cutters have worked.

Three days after leaving Paris the Gaileys had, sensibly, long returned to the warmth of a hotel room. It was still bitterly cold. It was below freezing most nights, we had ice on the deck every morning, and it was a good day when the air temperature climbed into the low 40°s F. The ripped sprayhood did little to combat the wind chill factor, and it was doubly unfortunate to be caught in a Siberian airstream in a boat built for the tropics. *Terrapin*, intentionally, had no form of heating. The aft cabin hatches were designed to keep out rain but also to allow a permanent cooling airflow, encouraged by deckhead extractor solar fans. We stuffed the hatches with towels. The only way to warm the main cabin was to light the stove, and suffer the condensation of a water laden atmosphere worse than a rain forest. Neither of us had the right clothes. Oh, we had silks and thermal vests, sailing underclothes and foul weather gear, but nothing for such continuous low temperatures and although we layered, it seemed our body core temperatures were slowly falling past resuscitation. The minuses, to be honest, were starting to outweigh the pluses. Negotiating each lock was fraught with peril, a test of endurance the like of which we'd never imagined. I hadn't thought it through. It was one thing going through the locks with Martyn. Either of us could take a line or take the wheel. Admittedly my boat handling was blind luck, rather than skill, for I still wasn't used to *Terrapin*, let alone the characteristics of a boat that floated on the water rather than in it, was almost square (or so it seemed) and whose twin engines and deep rudders could produce extraordinary results, like an instant 180° turn in your own length in midstream or have you heading straight for the bank as you reached for a mug of coffee. Janet, perhaps wisely, opted out of the driving. But it did mean that she saddled herself with all the line work, enough pulling and heaving to satisfy a California fitness freak, and with the job spec of deckhand went the task of leaping for the shore like a powder monkey as we entered each lock. The strange psychology of the business of boating began to make its mark. It wasn't quite a Bligh-Christian scenario, but there were moments when Janet's reluctance to jump three or four feet for a slimy iron ladder on a sheer lock wall, when I reckoned we faced imminent disaster if she didn't make it, introduced a new *frisson* into our relationship.

We were saved by another pair of hands. We were joined by Georgina Bates, my goddaughter 'George', who had given up temping in London for the delights of the French canals. Secretly briefed by Janet in a telephone call of desperation, she turned up with two hot water bottles, and enough pairs of heavy socks, thermals, gloves, and sweats to stock a disaster relief agency. We'd travelled some sixty miles and eight locks from Paris by then, and had lost our hearts to Samois-sur-Seine, the prettiest mooring place we'd yet found. It was there, while we paused in refuge waiting for George, that we were passed by another Heavenly Twins, *Floral Dancer*, making her way north. To our amazement they didn't stop, but swept on their way with the current. Where, we asked ourselves, was the comradeship of our small coterie of catamaran owners?

We turned off the Seine into the Yonne. By the time we reached Sens we'd discovered an undreamt of trial: a series of five locks with sloping sides, a specialty of the Yonne, which must have been designed as tests of manhood, if not as catamaran traps. We stopped for a brief period of recovery each lunch time, for sensibly the lockkeepers quit work then, and for an hour or two we huddled in the rain forest saloon, multi-socked feet on hot water bottles under the table, looking anxiously at the guide to see what new trials lay ahead. Janet must have been the first person to swim in the Yonne that year, when something didn't go quite right with the releasing of our lunchtime mooring lines. It was that day we discovered she was wearing all eight layers of the clothes she possessed, and I discovered that four of my toes were frostbitten. My fingers and thumbs were split open from handling cold, wet warps, and my hands were virtually crippled, useless for anything requiring dexterity. The canals of France, I reminded myself, were the 'dream route' to the Mediterranean. Janet put her views fairly succinctly in a postcard to a friend:

"So you think boating is fun . . . we have done 141 miles in 8 days (including 6 back). Police diver had to cut 100 yards of polyethylene from a propeller half an hour after leaving Paris. Tor got sick. George arrived. I fell into the river. We've grounded in shallow water and bashed the keels in sloping sided locks. Now one filter has gone in an engine and we wait for a spare. Temperature only 45°F and freezing at nights. No heating on the boat and nothing dries. Bitter cold. Other than that, great fun."

You might have said we were not entirely happy, but we were heading south and we were half way through April. The cold weather couldn't last. Could it? It was Good Friday, a Friday 13th admittedly, but our luck must surely change. It was time to take a decision about our route. There is only one way to reach the Mediterranean from Châlon-sur-Saône in central France, and that is to drop south down the River Saône to Lyon and go on, due south, straight down the Rhône to the coast; but earlier on, between Paris and Châlon, you have options. There are four ways you can go.

You can swing to the east and take the Marne and then the Canal de la Marne à la Saône. It's the longest route, but they say it's pretty. You can keep to the west, turn off the Seine into the Canal du Loing at St Mammes, and then take the Canal de Briare and the Canal Latéral à la Loire, and the Canal du Centre to Châlons. The first part of this route carries a lot of commercial traffic. In the centre you have two choices: at the start you turn off the Seine and take the Yonne to Joigny. The Canal de Bourgogne is the major route to the Saône, but there is an

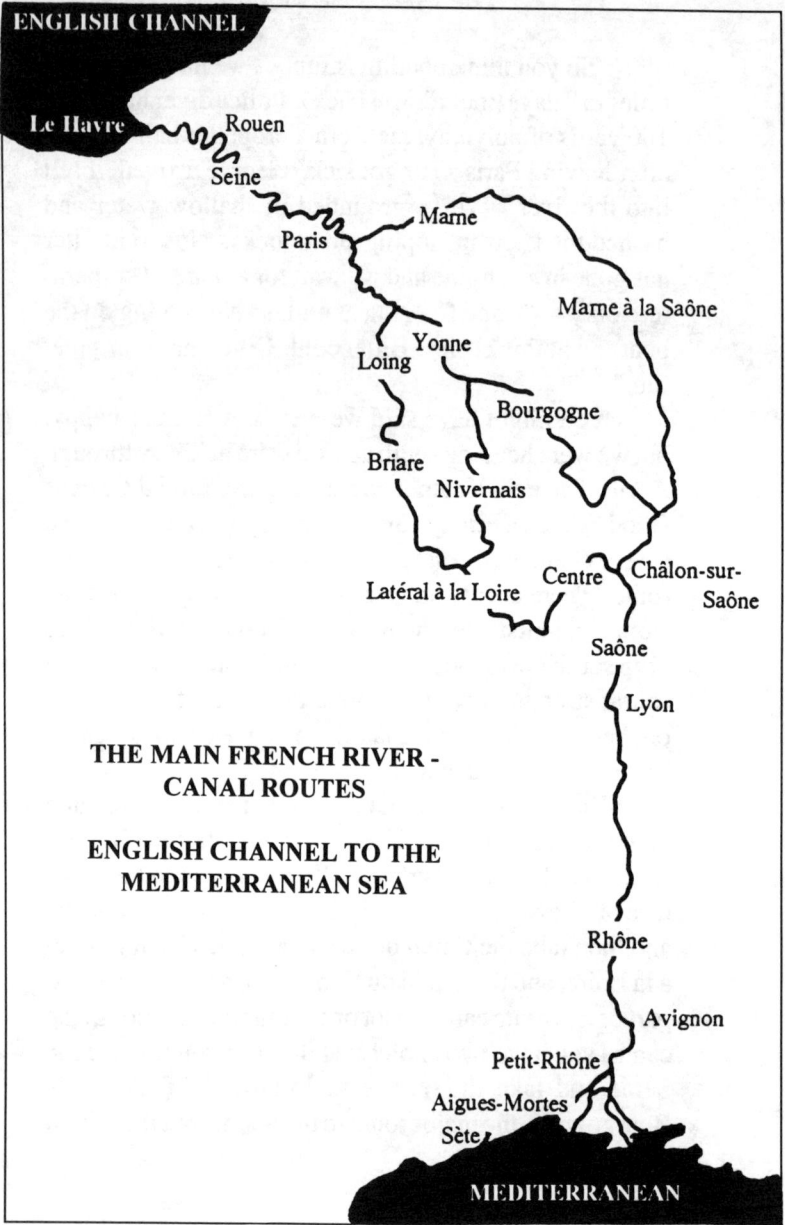

ENGLISH CHANNEL

Le Havre
Rouen
Seine
Paris
Marne
Marne à la Saône
Yonne
Loing
Bourgogne
Briare
Nivernais
Latéral à la Loire
Centre
Châlon-sur-Saône
Saône
Lyon

**THE MAIN FRENCH RIVER -
CANAL ROUTES**

**ENGLISH CHANNEL TO THE
MEDITERRANEAN SEA**

Rhône
Avignon
Petit-Rhône
Aigues-Mortes
Sète
MEDITERRANEAN

alternative, further up the Yonne: the Canal du Nivernais which starts at Auxerre. All accounts suggested that this was a sideline, used only by three-day hire boats, and it was certainly not a main route: too narrow? too shallow? As a final check we went through the *chomages*, the lists of annual canal maintenance closures, and no canal works were scheduled for April. We could take any route. We chose the Bourgogne. We spent Easter in mediaeval Joigny in heavy rain and high winds, glad that it was a holiday and the locks were closed, for there were white horses on the Yonne. By 1030 the next day we'd locked into the Canal de Bourgogne and by 1110 we were out again, back in the Yonne. Why? The Bourgogne was closed to through traffic. There was too little water at the higher levels. It was not a good start to the new beginning and the temperature was still only 42° F. What next? Unless we were going to backtrack for days, it could only be the Canal du Nivernais.

Five days later the tiny *Terrapin* looked huge in the upper locks of the Nivernais, dwarfing her surroundings as she floated high above the green fields and white Charolais cattle on her twin hulls, filling the narrow width of the ancient locks with barely nine inches to spare on each side. The scale had changed overnight and we were in an order of totally reversed magnitude from the locks of the Seine. It was almost like finding yourself in a toy world where everything was miniature, even the lockkeepers' cottages with their pocket handkerchief gardens, guardian geese, chicken runs, and small orchard paddocks with three or four sheep under the trees. The incongruity of it all was reinforced by the absence of any commercial canal traffic. Easter had produced a brief rash of holiday boats on the Yonne at Joigny and Auxerre, but it was still early in the season on the Nivernais. We were alone most of the time and in our isolation, *Terrapin*, against a backdrop of apple blossom and canal banks covered in cowslips, seemed mammoth and alien. A spaceship from another totally different civilization. "Ah" said one of the lady lock keepers, the *éclusiers*, having asked *Terrapin*'s destination. "*Vous venez en tel grand bateau* to make such a long voyage, and you come by our little canal?" She seemed amazed.

There were times when we too thought our progress was amazing. In the five days since we'd been turned away from the Canal de Bourgogne we'd got 50 miles further south, had another 42 locks and even a bascule bridge to our credit, and as far as canal lock-work was concerned, we'd pulled our act together. The adrenaline-stimulating early post-Paris days with dropped warps, near-collisions, and their constant potential for every imaginable kind of boating accident, were over and for the first time we started to have fun. We celebrated Janet's birthday at the Hotel de la Poste in Auxerre, the sun came out, the weather really was improving, and cock-a-hoop with the change we took the next two days at a run. You can't imagine how well organized we were. Janet or George would take one of our folding bikes and set off down the tow path, ahead, to warn the next lock keeper so that most times, rather than waiting for the lock to be filled and the gates opened for us, we could motor straight in. The powder monkey days were over too, for the bicyclist and the lock keeper were there to take lines. And there were other bonuses from having a hand on shore, fresh bread, local cheese, and red wine for lunch.

Crew morale went sky high. On one day we achieved 20 miles, 16 locks, and 6 bridges, and La Belle France was back into favor when Janet found a house which caught her heart, shuttered and forlorn, in a superb site between the river and the canal at St Didier. The climax of the Nivernais came with a test which would have shattered us in our earlier days, 36 locks, which included a final 'staircase' of fourteen connected locks to reach the watershed between the Yonne and the Loire, followed by three unlighted tunnels which took us through the divide. That day we covered only seventeen miles, but the mileage was nothing. We'd won through. We were in another country. Northern France was behind us, there were just forty miles to go before we reached the Loire. No more than 23 locks. Nothing. All descending locks. Anyone who has been through the canals of France will tell you descending locks are a cinch. No turbulence. You can take them single-handed with a single line.

We celebrated our successful navigation of the Nivernais that evening in a *bistro* in Marré in which, it seemed, half the village were celebrating something. The revelry was contagious. Oblivious of thunder, lightning, and rain we made our way back to the canal somewhat unsteadily to walk the plank to our beds. There we found two stray lambs on the towpath who had adopted *Terrapin* as a foster mother and refused to be parted from her. Their unbreakable loyalty to their new parent, demonstrated by continuous, incessant bleating, set the cap on the day. It was quite a night.

Janet and George stayed with *Terrapin* until we reached the junction of the Nivernais with the Loire at Decize. Years back, in my first planning, I'd hoped we might have reached Avignon before Janet had to return home, but the agonies of the cold weather days had set us back about a week. A day later it was another crew change as Harri Russell arrived with her backpack at Decize railway station for the run down the Saône and the Rhône to the Mediterranean. We had about a day and half to go on the Canal Latéral à la Loire before we reached the Canal du Centre at Digoin, which would take us directly to Châlon-sur-Saône. On the second day, as the lock gates opened just as we were about to leave the Ecluse de Theil, I thought I must be hallucinating. There, holding off, suspended between canal and sky in the morning calm, was our mirror image: a boat with unmistakable twin white hulls, a turtle-backed coachroof, and a yellow sprayhood. For the second time in *Terrapin*'s travels, we met another Heavenly Twins, *Festina Lente*, heading north like her cousin we'd met earlier. With barely twelve boats a year being built, *Terrapin*'s kith and kin are a rare breed and the odds are stacked against such chance encounters, but once again we passed without contact. I began to have grave reservations about the kind of people who bought Heavenly Twins.

We entered Digoin on the Pont-Canal, a superb eleven arch viaduct taking the captive canal high over the Loire between flagstone pavements, wrought iron railings and street lamps. It's quite an experience. Briare, further back up the western route, has a similar bridge-canal built by Gustave Eiffel. Two days later we reached Châlon-sur-Saône.

There's something about Châlon. You know it must be important because of its geography, because there you leave the small canals and there's nothing but the great rivers, the Saône and the Rhône ahead, super highways after twisting country lanes. You know it's a straight run to the south and you know the Med is only five days away, if you want to push it, and you look up and look around, and suddenly you realize the whole country-side has changed. Yes, you are in another part of France when you reach Châlon. We could tell it on our last day on the Canal du Centre between St Gilles and Chagny. There are no locks on that stretch, though you've still got twelve locks to go before you hit the Saône, and for the first time you have a chance to do something other than prepare your lines for the next lock. After days of myopia you can look around, for the first time there's depth and perspective, a distant whaleback ridge, closer hill slopes covered by vineyards, and the land has new colors, no longer the green of water meadows but the colors of the south, umber and terra-cotta. Harri sat on the foredeck drawing and I had my Walkman plugged into my ears with Bizet's *Pearl Fishers* playing. It would be hard to better the elation of that morning. The locks in that area are automatic, electrically controlled, and you activate the closing of the gates behind you by pulling a signal line. We'd got our drills so well rehearsed by then we could be through a lock, assuming we had it to ourselves, in five minutes. It could be an all-time record. But foolish vanity apart, it was the valiant *Terrapin* who deserved congratulation, for when we reached Châlon she'd clocked up her first thousand miles.

We stayed a full day in Châlon. It was May Day, May 1st. The locks were closed. It was good to have a break and even better to have a chance to think of sea matters again, splice in anchor rode markers (a long delayed task), fit safety harness and lifejackets, start looking at charts with a measure of concentrated interest and reread the South of France pilot. It took a day and a half to reach Lyon and we went straight through the city and reached Pierre-Bénite, the first lock on the Rhône, by midday. Once again the scale had changed dramatically. Everyone knows the Rhône locks are large but they still come as a shock: compared to them, the Seine locks rate as a play school. Faced by the immensity of these locks, anything up to 650 feet long by 40 feet wide with massive elliptical steel shutters rising like a solid portcullis at the far end, you feel like holding back. You hesitate at the presumption of taking anything as small and as frail as *Terrapin* into such a vast open basin, and you know that it is no seven foot Nivernais change of level that you are about to face but a drop of 60 to 85 feet, and something like two million cubic feet of water are let go when they pull the plug. What is almost unbelievable is that if there are no other ships travelling your way, they will activate these great locks for you alone, which means moving a mass of water that could float *QE 2* to meet the humble needs of a boat which could sit in the palm of your cupped hand. But you find you are let down so gently that if you had ice in your drink the cubes wouldn't even clink, and floating bollards take your lines down with you, in front of your eyes.

All you need worry about is the river itself. The chutes, the man-made cuts which bypass the worst stretches of the old, fierce Rhône, can be deceptive and there the current can boil in surprising eruptions, but your worst enemy is boredom. The long cuts are dreary; but they take you far on your way. The river itself is wide and deceptively calm, tamed into apparent docility by the superb engineering of the Compagnie Nationale du Rhône, but soon you realize that this is no gentle river, it's flowing and moving fast, way faster than you think. I woke up when we were going past a kilometer post every two and a half minutes, which made our speed over the ground almost 13 knots. Within two days we did eleven locks including the fabled Bollène, the archetype of Rhône locks, swept past one nuclear power station after another, Pierrelatte, Eurodif, the Centre d'Energie Atomique, with barely time to note their sinister common trademark, an immediate 10°-15° rise in river water temperature. Then we funneled through the Défilé de Donzère, the gorge south of Viviers, and were moored under the walls of Avignon, right by the famous bridge, the Pont St Bénézet, by mid-afternoon. It doesn't seem much in the telling, but look at a map of France. It was some run.

Martyn, quite unable to keep away, flew to Lyon, took the TGV, and rejoined *Terrapin* in Avignon. We spent a day seeing the Palais des Papes, climbing the Rocher des Doms, got lost in the labyrinthine streets of the old town, and could have stayed another day or even longer, but the call of the sea was strong. Four hours south of Avignon we reached the start of the Petit Rhône and turned into the flat marshland of the Camargue country. After the broad sweep and surfing exhilaration of the great river it was like taking a jungle creek, but there were other excitements for suddenly four wild colts burst out of the undergrowth onto the sand at the river's edge, racing each other, rearing and turning, totally oblivious of *Terrapin*'s pedestrian progress barely a tail's length from their playground.

You take the last lock of your journey through France when you turn off the Petit Rhône into your last canal, the Canal du Rhône à Sète, which takes you to Aigues-Mortes, a 13th Century time capsule, 'the most perfect old embrasured wall in France', with its fifteen towers and ten gates. The wetlands, salt pans, and the *etangs*, the inland seas, make it a dramatic place to approach by boat, the silhouette of the guardian walls and the great Tour de Constance visible from miles off, but the whole world seemed to be there by the time we reached the town and that was the end of any illusion of isolation. Aigues-Mortes, certainly that day, must have been the target of every bus tour in the region. Strangely, despite the crowds in the Place St Louis, there was no-one in Notre Dame-des-Sablons, the church where the great warrior saint Louis IX had prayed before setting out into the Mediterranean on his first crusade to Palestine, on the 25th August 1248. The church is beautiful in the stark simplicity of its bare stone, its only decoration the firefly flickering of the votive candles burning on great iron stands in the side aisles. There in the peace and quiet, conscious of the thousands of miles of ocean that lay ahead, I lit a candle and left it burning for *Terrapin*.

I'm not certain, as I look back, quite why I chose to enter the Mediterranean at Sète rather than Le Grau-de-Roi or Port Camargue on the doorstep of Aigues-Mortes. Someone had told me that Sète was the best place to get your mast stepped, which was bad advice and patent nonsense, but we didn't know it then, and so after a six hour run down the canal the next morning we eventually got there and found a mooring in the Vieux Bassin. Exactly 48 hours later we were ready to go to sea. Perhaps it's the right moment to reflect on the business of going through the French canals. I knew so little about it before we started, the few guidebooks I found were confusing if not intimidating, and failed to present any kind of overview of the undertaking so that you could understand what you were facing at the outset.

Terrapin had registered 1,288.2 nautical miles in Sète. We'd covered 1,030.67 miles from Chichester, with 33 days and 928.67 miles on the French canals. If you want to count the hurdles on the track, we'd passed through 258 locks, three tunnels, and seven self-operated opening bridges. Engine hours, purely on the canals, amounted to 233.88 hours or, to put it another way, we carried out our third oil change in Sète. What else can I usefully say? We'd spent eleven nights secured in *ports de plaisance* rather than going it alone on a canal bank or a quayside, and the mooring fees seemed to come out at roughly 60 francs a night, about $10, with Paris, hardly surprisingly, being the most expensive place. What do you get for your money? Water, sometimes a refuelling dock, showers, and somewhere to dump your garbage and your old engine oil. Not much, you could say, but the cost is hardly stunning and on the big rivers, as there are few places where it is safe to chance your arm and pull in to the bank, you have to find a marina. Some, like Châlon and Avignon, are superbly positioned in the heart of the ancient city and you are better sited there than you would be in any of the hotels. It's not easy to put a figure on the absolute cost of going through the canals. So much depends on your style of living, but obviously fuel is your major boat expense. We'd used 373.76 litres of diesel by the time we reached Sète which cost us 1,235 francs. $225. It was hardly outrageous.

Would I do the journey again? I don't know what the weather was doing in Biscay while we were in France and I guess it was foul there much of the time, but that apart, even offered the chance of a perfect offshore passage to Cádiz or Gibraltar, I'd choose to go by the French canals. Next time I'd like to take longer over it. I think two months would be perfect. Are there any drawbacks? Yes. If you are trying to press on, as we were, rather than dawdling through the canals, it can be quite a trial of endurance. If you happen to be the only person competent to maneuver into a lock, and hold the boat positioned inside the lock (for you keep your engines running) it can make for a long day at the helm, and you will have little chance to enjoy the scenery and do anything else other than drive the boat. The grit and grime that gets carried on board with the endless landings and re-embarkations at every lock, and every time you tie up against a bank, can be depressing, but I was probably new boat proud and fussy. The only answer is door mats. The kind of grit-shedders you can buy for a back door.

What other tips? Take every kind of connection in existence for your water hose and be prepared to fill your tanks jerrican by jerrican in places where the size and pipe thread of the local water supply still defeats you. Take a pair of folding bikes. They're essential for shopping, for fun, and for going ahead and setting up locks. Get a full set of canal guides. The French multilingual guides in the Carte Guide de Navigation Fluviale series by Michel Sandrin, with a single book devoted to each stretch of river or canal [published by Editions Cartographiques Maritimes, 7 Quai Gabrielle Péri, 7434 Joinville-le-Pont] are excellent. Take note that the canals are posted in kilometers so get a conversion scale to nautical miles worked out, and while you're at it, why not make a supplementary conversion table for those in the crew whose measurement of distance is more happily related to statute miles? Finally, remember that fuel is measured in litres, not gallons, and calculate your tank levels for refuelling.

Would I do the journey again? Yes. As Janet would say "You bet I would".

AND INTO THE MEDITERRANEAN

Sète, France, to Santa Pola, Alicante, Spain.
May 10 - 19 1990

Sète is not unattractive. You know without being told that the Phoenicians were there long before you and it has the sound provenance of being an ancient sea port, but I couldn't wait to get away. In part it was anger at being taken to the cleaners. We were not permitted to use the crane at the Club Nautique in the Vieux Bassin to raise our mast: we were told it was too difficult, there was every objection. It could have been done. At length a mobile crane was brought in, not at our bidding, and for a monstrous 600 francs ($110) we got our mast rigged. It leaves a bad taste. But the real motivation to get going was the Golfe du Lion and the weather. If you read the pilots, you would never contemplate sailing anywhere near the Gulf of Lions where sudden high winds, channelled into the Mediterranean by the Alps, the Massif Central, and the Pyrenees, can turn a flat calm into a Force 8 storm within fifteen minutes with no warning. You are advised that if you cannot find immediate shelter, you should seriously consider running ashore deliberately rather than sit it out, for bad weather there, which is always vicious, can last for days. We stood on the sea wall by the plaque that marks where the Israel-bound Exodus migration had left in 1947 and looked out over a calm sea. The forecast was that it would freshen to 25 knot winds from the north west sometime in the next 48 hours. There was a slow moving low somewhere, the weather was unsettled, there might be isolated thunder-storms. It was vague to the point of uselessness. One thing was certain. The calm couldn't last.

We left the moment we were ready. I might have become soft on the canals, but I had a fear of the Golfe du Lion like a knot of tarred twine in the pit of my stomach, and I wanted to get through it and out, on our way to Ibiza, about 400 miles away. It would have been nice to have been able to head for Ibiza as a straight shot, but in Sète we were too far to the west already and our initial course had to take us safely past Cap Béar and the Cabo de Creus on the Franco-Spanish border. After that we could turn south down the Costa Brava and set a new course to make a landfall on the north west coast of Mallorca, before turning for the Isla de Tagomago and Ibiza. By midnight the first night we were thirteen miles off Cape Béar, motorsailing, for the wind was only Force 2 and hanging around that coast just waiting for the weather to change, right in the lion's mouth, seemed suicidal. The next three hours were nightmarish. We came upon an armada of fishing boats and bewildering necklaces of bright lights running out into the sea. I had the uneasy feeling that we were about to get tied up in the biggest set of tuna nets in Spain, and the best thing to do was to get well away and set a course for Ibiza later. By dawn we were fine. By 1030 the weather had changed completely, we had the cruising chute up for the first time and a school of porpoises found *Terrapin* and stayed with us for an hour, leading us on our way. Six hours later there was a flat, oily calm underlaid by a long swell from the south and we went back to motor sailing. And so it went on, for much of the next day, the Med as fickle and as changeable as it's always reputed to be.

We sighted Mallorca just before midday on Saturday, forty eight hours after setting out. With barely 30 miles to go to our first waypoint in the Balearic Islands the wind kicked up from the west and all we could do was alter course and run to the south east so that we could, hopefully, take a long tack in to Puerta Ibiza. In the way in which misfortune can multiply at sea, something went wrong that night and by 2300 we were lost. *Terrapin* was being thrown around, sleeping was impossible, the GPS satellites were below the horizon, and there wasn't a star in sight. For the last six hours the log was blank. Nothing but guesswork, you couldn't call it dead reckoning, brought us within the loom of the light on Tagomago and once we had that, we were home. We arrived in Puerto Ibiza Nueva at 0720, perhaps more tired than we ought to have been, after a passage of 382 miles from Sète.

GPS, undoubtedly the only navigation system worth considering today, is a potentially hazardous siren but even a Ulysses might be tempted to place absolute faith in the system. It's so easy to rely on it for every answer. It was, I think, a timely lesson to have fitted *Terrapin* with GPS before its satellite deployment was complete, for given the luxury of full-time coverage I could see my feeble skills in conventional navigation eroding for lack of exercise. It's so easy to forget that batteries can go flat and gremlins, against all probability, can invade and take over black boxes at any time. It was good to find that my sights, other than the bad ones that put us in the South Pacific or the Indian Ocean, placed us within five miles of the GPS position, but in the blackness of that last night there was no backup. It was then that I realized two things. The first was that every compass on *Terrapin*, the ST-50 fluxgate, the autopilot, the Plastimo Contest, my binoculars, and my Mini 2000, were in disagreement. Not very reassuring. It was the direct product of a rushed and badly organized commissioning. My second realization was that my store-bought log book was useless. I thought I'd chosen the best of them; but unless the pages of your log reflect the way you are navigating, your instruments, and the order in which information comes up, you end up with the log ignored, working off scraps of paper with the last fix scribbled on a Post It note stuck on the edge of the saloon table. Better customize your log. Even better, design your own.

We stayed two days in Ibiza, for what is the point in sailing somewhere exotic only to press on at once? My original plan had been to end the first leg in Gibraltar and leave *Terrapin* there for the summer, simply because it was English-speaking and on the threshold of the Atlantic. I changed my mind. We were a week or more behind my target schedule, not that it mattered, but we were hitting crew limits. Martyn was beginning to feel that he had run out of play time, and Harri had taken all the time she could from her art school. It seemed sensible in any event to start off again in October with at least a week or so of Mediterranean sailing, just in case something needed fixing, rather than taking straight off into the Atlantic where the distance between ports was greater. I looked at the map when we reached Ibiza, for such decision-making hangs on the location of international airports.

Alicante? Malaga? It was May 13th and I would need about 3-4 days to put *Terrapin* to bed for the summer. I chose Alicante. That gave us something like 120 miles to go from Ibiza. About 21 hours? Make an early start and get in around midnight? Or sail through the night and arrive in daylight?

We left at dawn on May 15th. I made the wrong choice. I wanted daylight for our passage between Ibiza and Formentera and reckoned that arriving off Alicante at night would present no problems for it would be well marked. It was still daylight when we made our landfall off Calpe, just south of the Cabo de la Nao, but Benidorm was a string of lights as we passed, the chart took no account of tourist development, and the navigation lights I wanted were swamped in the glare and glitter of the Costa Blanca. It took half a lifetime before I located the Cabo de la Huertas, the leading light as you approach Alicante from the north. Then it was fine. We had no real problems other than a dredger parked in the main entrance to the harbor with two unlit attendant barges standing off from it, and what appeared, at first sight, to be a full inner harbor with no place for a visitor to lodge for the night. But by two in the morning we were secure against a wall; and then we opened our last bottle of Avignon *rosé*.

There was no place to leave *Terrapin* in Alicante. The one yard with a travel hoist reckoned her beam was over their limits and I didn't want to leave her in the water, even if there was a vacant berth in the inner harbor: Alicante was too big a port, too busy, too impersonal, and there was no secluded area for yachts. There was no

37

option but to move on and keep looking for somewhere better. Harri got a flight to London, and Martyn and I sailed on that afternoon. Two hours later we found the perfect place in Santa Pola. The Vatasa yard was just the right size, remote enough from Santa Pola itself for the right degree of privacy, and they had a travel hoist. Within an hour *Terrapin* was out of the water sitting on her keel shoes. I'd dreaded seeing her beneath the waterline, half-convinced that the bottom of her rudders would be shredded and her hulls scarred by the awful days in the sloping locks of the Yonne, but she looked almost as good as new. There was one scratch on the port side, deeper than I cared for, but I knew about that, for it was entirely my fault. Like a great idiot I'd run into the bank on the Canal du Centre while looking at the guide-book rather than where I was going. We stayed on *Terrapin* working on her until it was too dark to see and guessing that we'd go out to find supper somewhere, the old night watchman came round to introduce his two German shepherd dogs to us so that we wouldn't be eaten alive when we bicycled back to the yard from Santa Pola.

The next morning Martyn left and I stayed on, finishing cleaning, getting laundry done in a local *lavandería*, and doing everything that you have to do for a boat that has come a long way and has been your home for some time. I had been living on board for eight weeks by then, and *Terrapin* had logged over 1,500 nautical miles since we left Chichester. The first leg was over. There was much to be done before starting again in October. The sprayhood had to be repaired, and I wanted to remake the bimini before setting out into the Atlantic.

My original design, intended to double as a water catchment, was not satisfactory. There were, as always, lists to take away: needed tools, spare parts, fishing gear, missing comforts, the next set of charts and pilots, and new provisioning lists. And sometime during the summer I was determined to use my computer to design and print what I reckoned would be the ideal form for a log. But in Santa Pola at the end of May there was nothing more to be done.

On Saturday afternoon May 19th I flew from Alicante to London on the first stage of my way back to the States. I felt strangely disoriented in the check-in line up at Alicante airport and, as we took off and circled over the coast just north of Santa Pola, I felt suddenly, totally, and completely bereft leaving *Terrapin*.

BARREN CAPES
AND YARDS OF PLASTIC

Santa Pola to El Puerto de Santa Maria, Cádiz Bay.
October 23 - November 13 1990

On October 23rd 1990 Alicante looked golden, brilliant in the midday sun. The Mediterranean was blue and turquoise, with ripples that would have hardly set a plastic duck in motion. It was reassuring, more so flying in from a cold, damp, autumnal England already lashed by the first storms of winter. I'd feared that I might have left my return too late. Victoria, veteran of the arctic April in Paris, now graduated from Cambridge and taking a half term break from Law School in London, was with me. Between us we had eleven pieces of baggage ranging from a vegetable rack to six two-gallon plastic water cans, which somehow we'd persuaded the airline came within their limit of two bags per passenger. The day after our arrival in Santa Pola, Martyn flew in, having taken a week off boat-building to help *Terrapin* set out on the second stage of her journey.

Where was I going? So much depended on the weather. Gibraltar certainly. Further than that if possible. I'd decided to return to Vermont for Thanksgiving and Christmas, take a break, and set out again in early January on the long haul which would keep me on *Terrapin* for four months, so I was not trying to achieve much more than 500 miles on this leg. My positioning at the end was all important, ideally it had to be somewhere on the Atlantic coast ready for a straight run to the Canaries. Cádiz? Or go up the Guadalquivir to Seville?

41

Or go on for another two days to Vilamoura? But the further you travel out along the Atlantic coast the further north you will go, losing precious miles won heading south towards the sun on the Mediterranean side. The basic requirement, to my mind, was to get clear of the Strait of Gibraltar for if the weather was adverse there, you could be holed up in Gib for a week or more waiting for fair winds. Beyond that, I wanted to hold on to my Distance South Made Good, to keep within the same band of latitude as Tarifa, the southernmost tip of Spain, which was 36°N. In effect this set a limit of no further north than Cádiz Bay, and despite the attraction of Seville, I left it at that. Open ended.

Months later I worked out that it always seemed to take no more and no less than exactly three days to prepare *Terrapin* for sea, and three days to put her to bed at the end of a passage. We'd flown in to Alicante at midday on Tuesday and by midday on Friday we had *Terrapin* back in the water, moving and alive again as we ran all of a mile and a half across the bay to the Club Nautico in Santa Pola to spend a night there. Victoria left reluctantly to fly back to London the next morning in the dawn of another perfect day, the attraction of a career in law fading against the magnetism of voyaging south, the terrible compulsion to forget everything and sail on.

Martyn and I set out on our first leg and took immediate delight in hitting 6.7 knots right at the start. Then the wind shifted 180° at noon and we were forced to motor. It was back, as ever, to the fickle Med. My Atlantic sailing companions to be, Phil Hoskins and Nikki Pendry, were wintering in their Heavenly Twins,

Two Minds, at the Marina Internacional in Torrevieja. We had agreed, tentatively, that we'd take *Terrapin* across the Atlantic together in early 1991 but nothing was set in concrete, so Torrevieja was a vital first stop after leaving Santa Pola. Above this, I had crew problems. Martyn had two days remaining before he was due to fly out from Alicante, and my Mediterranean crew list, once he left, was nothing but a string of broken promises. At least in Torrevieja for the first time, after being cold-shouldered twice on the French canals, *Terrapin* was alongside one of her own kith and kin. There, possibly overcome by it all, Martyn decided to stay until we reached Cartagena and I decided that I'd sail on single-handed once he'd left, hopping from port to port in fair weather. Phil and Nikki consulted. Nikki had a job in Torrevieja which she wanted to keep until just before Christmas, but Phil had finished laying up *Two Minds* for the winter. He'd sail with *Terrapin.* You could call it a pre-Atlantic work-up.

We set out the next morning under full sail with Nikki waving us off when inside five minutes, after a deceptive start as a gentle breeze, the wind whammed us at 35 knots out of a clear blue sky. Nikki had a grandstand view as we went through every shorten sail drill as if making a textbook video. After working like demented octopi for a few frantic minutes, with Phil clearly worried about Nikki's peace of mind, we disappeared in a lather of whitecaps heading south under the staysail. But it was the same old story. No wind by 1100, then back to Force 4-5, and then we were slamming into heavy seas and it was obvious that trying to force our way around the Cabo de Palos would have been crazy.

We turned and ran for the Puerto de Tomás Maestre, the entry point to the Mar Menor, the Costa Blanca's great inland sea, and miraculously caught the swing bridge over the entry canal at its afternoon opening time. The wind was still Force 4 inside the Mar Menor although the sea state was much reduced without the fetch of the open Med, and we motor sailed for the Puerto de los Nietos on the southern shore, practicing the deployment of our Man Overboard equipment on the way. The Danbuoy and horseshoe lifebuoy, with their self-activating lights, hit the water reluctantly after an interminable delay and the whole launching apparatus, designed to be operated instantly by whoever was on watch in the cockpit, failed dismally. Recovering everything we found a critical securing strap on the horseshoe buoy, which had been made fast by nothing more than a single letter-size staple, had parted. It was manufacturing negligence, I thought, grave enough to justify a lawsuit, but at least we discovered this when no life was at stake. We entered the Puerto de los Nietos and incredibly there, alongside the only vacant berth, was another Heavenly Twins. Not in truth a pretty vessel, the curiously named *Onions*, much modified, august in age, was a cousin to *Terrapin* none the less. There was no trace of *Onions*'s owners.

Martyn left for Alicante on a village bus the next morning and by midday Phil and I were off the Cabo de Palos, conscious that the weather was worsening. As we rounded the cape the wind was up to 19 knots, but far worse was a heavy swell topped with a lot of wave and everything was coming right on the nose, which catamarans certainly don't like and most sensible sailing people would avoid. We headed for the closest port, the tiny Puerta de la Espada right under the Cabo de Palos, which was there, all too close and almost under our right elbows as we were being thrown around. The East Spain Pilot suggested that we could enter even under those conditions and that we'd be safe inside, so rather than run back for shelter on the northern side of the cape, we turned in to land. I've never had such a hellish approach with breakers on an offshore reef, non-existent buoys, a 180° turn into the entrance channel while still exposed to both wind and wave, and a further 90° turn into the harbor itself. And there was no space in there. Was it the weather? The harbor was full. A *marinero* met us and, despite our entreaties, refused to let us raft alongside anyone else. Not overly concerned with the fortunes of one small foreign play boat, he offered us the side wall in the entrance channel. It was getting close to a real worry situation. Outside it was almost too rough to consider putting out again with safety; if anything went wrong, we would be wrecked within minutes. Inside the entrance channel we were protected to a point, but the outer mole had arched water channels cut through it for some inexplicable reason and the surge inside the channel was appalling. We used the two French canal car tires we'd saved to use as sea brakes as fenders, but even then we were thrown against the wall time and time again with the kind of force that can destabilize your cocktail hour and come close to spoiling your evening, and all the while the wind was howling in the rigging. It made for a poor night. Then just before dawn it quieted. And when we left later in the morning almost desperate, given the chance, to get away from that hellish sanctuary, there was still a heavy swell running. The wind was down to 3 knots: but there are times when nothing is quite perfect. It was still right on the nose. But we were out, we were at sea, and we could breathe again.

We decided to skip Cartagena. Phil and Nikki had been there in *Two Minds* during the summer. "Worst berth we've ever had" he said. "Too busy, the Spanish Navy going in and out all day and all night, wash the whole time, and too big a city. Parts of it OK, but just too much of a big city". We settled for Mazarrón, 40 miles from Puerta de la Espada. We wanted a chance to buy bread, milk, and fresh vegetables and we wanted a night's rest. It seemed that our stars were not in the ascendant on that section of our passage south. The Puerta de Deportivo de Mazarrón charged catamarans double the normal boat rate, despite the fact that our beam was less than that of many of the monohulls paying 'single' rates. The marina showers and washing facilities were locked and remained obstinately locked. The only supermarket was miles away from the marina and all the local small shops were closed, for the next day was a Saints Day, which, if your approach to the business of living is to expend minimal energy, was a cogent reason for abandoning work the day before.

Our neighbor, a 43 ft Bénéteau Océanis flying a Red Ensign, appeared to our amazement to be crewed by an elderly lady, patently the grandmother of a precocious little girl of ten or eleven, who was the only other member of the yacht's complement. Granny was scrubbing the decks with extraordinary dedication and, for a brief moment, her granddaughter took a break from an endless stream of supervisory advice and comment to tell us what was going on: "My daddy and my mummy are coming but we don't know when they'll arrive. Mummy has a baby. She's my sister but she's very small. We think they'll be coming by taxi. We're going to go shopping, aren't we, Granny, to get some things before they arrive when we've finished cleaning the boat. We've got a lot of things to do, haven't we, Granny? We got here first." The final remark was added proudly. So when Granny was released from her foredeck work we all walked in to the town together and found the supermarket about forty minutes after we started out. I couldn't think how our neighbors would make it back to the marina with any kind of worthwhile load, but Granny reassured me. They would be all right. They'd take a taxi. Phil and I backpacked a staggering haul of heavyweight essentials and found when we unpacked that we'd achieved little more in our restocking than adding another two cans of tuna to a stock which already looked as if we'd cornered the tuna market, one can of calamaries to the two we already had on *Terrapin*, and enough water and wine to flood a dry dock. But we did remember to get a fresh loaf of bread.

Our friends stayed on shopping. We must have missed their return in our preoccupation with cooking an evening meal, but much later that night we heard Mummy and Daddy arrive. Yes, it was true. Mummy had a sleeping baby in her arms and Mummy was looking out of sorts and tired. She also appeared to be suffering from some form of recreational disorientation or delusion, for she was braceleted and bangled and dressed to the nines. She could have swept with élan into the lobby of La Bobadilla and carried the day in any five star resort. Surely her shoes weren't heels, or were they? "Oh God" she said after getting on board with some difficulty "not down these bloody steps. I can see this is going to be bloody awful". No 1 daughter, wisely, was silent for the first time since we'd met her. Even Granny had clammed up. Daddy, sensibly inspecting and fiddling with his mooring lines, kept very distant. The next morning Precocious escaped from the family breakfast and came to see us, just as we were preparing to leave. She was breathless with news. "We were very naughty last night" she confided. "Do you know what we did? We couldn't get a taxi, so we took our trolley from the supermarket and Granny pushed it all the way back here." I reckon that put Granny in the front rank of potential contenders for the Iditarod Dog Sled Race if nothing else, and I just hope M&D (who had yet to surface in the cockpit) really thanked her for her sterling work in recommissioning their boat. They left just after us, heading north. But by then the wind had changed completely: we were running at 6.6 knots in 16 knots of wind as we settled on 210° and they had it right in the teeth as they set their course for the Cabo de Palos. I've often wondered how they got on.

It was November 1st. Perhaps the change of month did it, or perhaps it was the full moon on the 2nd, but for four days it all went swingingly. Oh, the Med was changeable, but we got some good sailing in and the wind favored us much of the time. That first day out of

Mazarrón we made it to Garrucha and achieved 7.5 knots under sail, which was our best speed so far. The next day we bit off another bite sized chunk and selected San José as our stopping place. It turned out to be one of those places that are exactly right and, if we hadn't been in the business of getting to Gibraltar without undue delay and out into the Atlantic, I would have stayed on. The set of the coast and the pocket town were just as you thought a place on the Costa Blanca should be: the little harbor was the right size, it had a couple of restaurants, the walk into the town round the small bay and the curve of a sand beach, was just enough exercise and not too punishing a distance under the now common backpack loads of liter bottles of water and, yes, liter bottles of local wine. And it was a full moon night. What more could you ask for? But I was glad that we were not there in the full flush of the tourist season. It could be, and I'm sure it is, very different then.

The next morning, as if a note of caution was necessary, we had a total screw-up leaving the harbor. Mediterranean mooring stern on to the quayside (in fact we always went bows in) is an admirable space-saver, but there are drawbacks. The getting in was never difficult, unless it was unduly tight and the wind was overly strong, but the system has its hazards. If there's a *marinero* waiting ready to hand you the stern line which he's already picked up, there are no problems. You can take it aft and make it secure, distancing your bows from the wall as you wish, and you're there. All set. If you have to fish for the line with a boat hook, it can become more interesting. I don't know that I would have liked to hold a single engined boat poised for five minutes while the fishing for that vital line went on, for occasionally it seemed to take that long. *Terrapin* certainly won on her twin screw agility. You never needed to touch the wheel and it was probably better if you didn't. You could do everything with the engines alone, even to the point of going into a crowded marina and making a circuit of it searching for a vacant berth. But what about the leaving? As I said, we got it wrong in San José.

We dropped the stern line well clear before we reversed, but unknown to us its tensioning snapped it across the starboard propeller as the line sank to the bottom. Two minutes later *Terrapin* was hog-tied in the main channel with the starboard engine out of action, tethered to the great lump of mooring that had held us the night before. Even worse, the continuity of the line to its terminal mooring ring on the quay side no longer existed, for the propeller had cut it. Two fishing boats swept past us heading out into the bay, little concerned with our apparent hesitation in going their way, and a large black inflatable packed with men dressed in suits sped off on some curious mission. We couldn't turn. We couldn't, on the length of our underwater tether, even make the quay. Forty five minutes later we left in our normal style leaving a grateful *marinero*, who by then had seen us and guessed that something had gone wrong, with a newly joined mooring line. He seemed little concerned that we had severed it in the first place. There was a shrug of the shoulders. It often happened. That's Mediterranean mooring. And I promised Phil that I would do the diving the next time.

The Spanish coast is a succession of great bights separated by cape after cape, and point after point. The next of the Mediterranean capes, the Cabo de Gata, which marks the dividing line between the Costa Blanca and the Costa del Sol, was in sight from the time we left San José. In the curious way in which these things sometimes happen, we were there rounding the Cabo de Gato at 0830 and, as we altered course, *Terrapin*'s log registered exactly 2,000 nautical miles. It was a little like a birthday falling on the right day of the week. We broke our 'no alcohol while under way' rule and had a glass of *tinta* to celebrate the 2,000 and the fact that Gibraltar was then just 155 miles ahead. We wanted to visit the Marina del Este on the way, for it was supposed to be a stunning new development, but it was too far to take as one shot day sailing so we decided to make Almerimar as a half way point. Our putting out to sea and our coming into port were fated that day, for entering Almerimar both propellers became fouled with plastic. In a sense we'd seen it coming. My log entry made after the Cabo de Gato expresses some displeasure at our first sight of the Costa del Sol:

> "Costa Plastica! Bare, eroded hills and mountains. No vegetation other than scrub bushes. Endless 'greenhouses' on the coast - crops grown under hundreds of yards of plastic sheeting - grey, opaque. The world to come? And the endless developments . . ."

Barren Capes and Yards of Plastic

The Costa del Sol is not a pretty coast. You could say that it offers a graphic illustration of every conceivable mistake that could be made in littoral development. There is nothing there but the horrors of Man. Real horrors. Those bare hillsides. Were there ever trees there? Did the Phoenicians start to cut them down? Did the Arabs complete the hatchet work, or was the need to build merchant hulls and warships for the new kingdom of Spain the final blow? And who on earth is going to keep buying apartments on that coast, each new building shading its neighbors as well as eclipsing the sun totally from their much vaunted, fabled beaches by mid-afternoon each day. I cleared the propellers in Almerimar. Luck was with me, for I managed to get the plastic unwound with the boat hook. It took some time, but it was preferable to diving. The harbor was filthy.

It was a comfortable 53 miles to the Marina del Este and we had the cruising chute up for much of the time on our way there, but still lost the wind twice. After my condemnation of development along the Costa del Sol, I would give the Marina del Este, the Puerto de la Mona, a gold star. It is close to perfection: a deliberately limited development set against a promontory in which an offshore island has been incorporated into the outer harbor wall and all the houses have been set low, and low profile, around the little port. Four fifths of the available land has been left to nature, but a nature assisted, this time, by the planting of trees and flowering shrubs, which have been wisely left to grow in apparent natural chaos rather than in an alien urban discipline. If you were ultra-critical you could suggest that it was all very like a stage set, and so it was: but I would still give them that gold star. We wanted to time our arrival in Gibraltar for around midday rather than at the end of a day, so we selected Cabo Pino, just 57 miles from the Marina del Este, as our next stopping place which would leave 44 miles to be covered the next day. The Marina del Este was the final treat, really the only treat, of the Costa del Sol. During the day the weather worsened, the wind got up and the swell built up, and when we reached Cabo Pino it was the pits. We paid 1,225 pesetas (325 more than the Marina del Este) for nothing. There were no showers, no facilities whatsoever, and no supermarket or store within reasonable reach.

At least at Cabo Pino we were within VHF radio range of Gibraltar and for the first time we could get weather forecasts. I might well have suffered from finger trouble trying to tune both our FM/AM radio and the SSB during our Mediterranean passage, but it was either my lack of skill or that is the way it was, for up to that point we had never managed to get one intelligible weather forecast that was any use to us. We relied on the weatherfax maps that were sometimes posted in the better marinas, and, weather maps or not, we set out each day with our bad weather diversions already marked and the necessary waypoints plotted. But it was, I must admit, a relief to hear an English language marine forecast for the first time. It was not reassuring:

"... a falling low over Morocco to Portugal.
Wind easterly 5 to 6 rising to 6 to 7 in the
Strait and gale 8 in the afternoon. Visibility

good. Sea moderate to rough, and very
rough in the Strait . . ."

That was at 0645. By 1230 we'd had Gibraltar in
sight for an hour and a half, looking just like a great
whalebacked island, and the forecast was updated:

". . . Wind easterly 6 to 8 increasing to 9 in
the Strait. Visibility fair. Sea moderate to
very rough . . ."

It did seem to be a bit grey and it was rather like
riding a switchback by then. We had 23 knots of apparent
wind but it was favoring us and we were making 7 knots
under the genoa alone, with a Red Ensign and a Q flag
flying straight out under the starboard spreader as if they
were painted on boards. The Autohelm was fine but it
seemed better to steer, at least it made us feel that we were
sailing the boat rather than being sailed, and so we took
turns at the wheel. The sea state didn't seem to be that
formidable. Every now and again a wall of water raced
past us, but we were OK. Looking behind us I was glad
that there was no question of heading that way. At 1400
we were off Europa Point and we went round it like a car
on a skid pan, and then rolled in the genny. We started the
engines as we had an ebb tide to buck and black garbage
sacks, loose plastic, debris, and an endless stream of
urban detritus was already being carried past us. Fifteen
minutes later we lost the starboard engine. Plastic.
Around a propeller. Again. I was in luck for the
Almerimar boat hook excision worked a second time and
I cleared it, hanging over the side upside down in my
harness. We motored on towards the airport runway and

the marinas, the ebb tide still carrying its filth, with a blanket of grey cloud hanging low overhead. I had thought we would be well protected in the lee of the Rock but violent downdrafts of wind hit Gibraltar Bay like bomb blasts, and *Terrapin* shuddered under attack as we ploughed on. It was not for long. By 1430 we were at the Reporting Dock, cleared in, and twenty minutes later we were secure in Sheppard's Marina.

It was Tuesday November 6th. We spent the whole of the next day having a 500 hour service done on the engines, and left on Thursday morning. The storm had abated and we had a window of opportunity to get through the Strait and out into the Atlantic. The weather was foul the whole time we were in Gibraltar: low cloud, high winds, and incessant, drenching rain. The Rock was not attractive under such conditions, but I am not certain that it is attractive whatever the weather. As a visiting 'yachtie' I think Gibraltar suffers from too much custom from our kind. What is it? Over 5,000 yachts a year? Maybe it's up to the 8,000 mark now. Certainly the rise in recent years has been astronomic. Neither Sheppard's, nor the newer Marina Bay marina, can cope adequately with such a traffic flow on anything like a personal basis. So everything is rushed, take it or leave it, done without any real interest or real concern, simply a commercial act in return for money, and the ability to offer service has long been overtaken by potential demand. The Autohelm agent told me that he couldn't help me with a calibration problem for 8-10 days. The reason is, of course, that Gibraltar is a choke point. You have to go there if the weather is foul. If you're English-speaking, you're bound to be drawn there by that alone. Yes, Gibraltar does have agencies for almost every known name in marine equipment and it does have an international airport. But is there anything else, anything that might make you want to come back? I think not. The harbor is unbelievably dirty. The streets are dirty. There are far too many cars. Unless they're pressing the sale of so-called duty free goods, the local population has inherited many of the least attractive British traits, an unwillingness to put out, a near total absence of interest or empathy, and a contentment with poor service, lack of facilities, and restaurants that are as bad as most British ones were twenty five years ago. To add to my compilation of disappointment and indignation, the washing facilities offered by Sheppard's Marina were disgraceful by any standard. The worst I had yet seen.

I was in the office at Sheppard's Marina on the afternoon of our arrival trying to arrange our 500 hour engine service when my name was called out in incredulous surprise behind me. It was Tom Lowther, a friend of our son Edward, who I had last seen in Paris just three weeks before when we had said our good-byes at 0430 in the morning outside the Locomotion, a much in-vogue Pigalle disco. We'd been weekending in Paris celebrating Edward's birthday the week before I left for Alicante. Our meeting was a total surprise. Tom had just arrived in Gibraltar determined "to sail in the ARC or find a boat going to America that wanted a crewman". When had he arrived? That very morning. Despite the foul weather, he'd made his way at once to Europa Point because it was famous, and he wanted to look across the Strait to Africa.

He couldn't see anything of Africa but while he was there just one boat, a catamaran, came tearing round the corner, pulled its sails in, and turned up towards the harbor. What color was the sprayhood? Yellow. "I don't believe it. That's unreal. Was that you, then?" Later, that night, we persuaded Tom that he'd probably missed the mainstream of the westbound traffic, and that most of the ARC boats would be in the Canaries by then, or on their way there. His best chance would be to fly to the Canaries and see if anyone needed an extra hand, for someone might have to withdraw as crew for some reason and by the ARC rules each boat had to have a minimum of three on board. Failing that, he could sail with us for a day or so. He might find something in Cádiz. He'd tried Gibraltar already. There was nothing.

The three of us set out on Thursday morning, first taking on 62 litres of diesel. The tide was against us at the start but in our favor later, and I reckoned we could make Barbate de Franco, about 30 miles up the Atlantic coast north of Tarifa. The weather report sounded OK: a moderate SE wind, becoming southwesterly later. It would suit us well. We were shadowed through the Strait by a Spanish destroyer, a low black silhouette with a tall stack moving slowly against the mass of Jebel Musa, Gibraltar's twin peak, and the jagged backdrop of the Moroccan coast, and we made slow progress for the wind wasn't quite right and the tide seemed to take forever to turn. We favored the Spanish coast and our Red Ensign had long disappeared below to be replaced by the red and yellow colors of Spain on the signal halyard.

By 1445 we were approaching Tarifa and it was apparent that the forecast bore no relation to actuality. Heavy seas were breaking on the rocks of Punta de Tarifa and the moderate southwesterly had turned into a singularly immoderate northwesterly with a lot of squalls and a heavy swell. It really was 'Good-bye Mediterranean' and 'Hello Atlantic' as we rounded Tarifa into the teeth of it and the coastline became totally obscured in heavy rain. Our intended course took us close to an area of shoals, tide rips, and overflows which was not entirely relaxing under those conditions. By the time the wind was up to 20 knots, and still increasing, and the swells were somewhere around 8 ft, the fun element had gone out of the day's sailing. Tom had taken his first experience of ocean sailing without complaint, but his stoicism cracked with his evident relief when we turned and ran back to Tarifa.

Some day someone will develop Tarifa. The port, on the face of it, is fine: a ferry service to North Africa operates from there and the Spanish Navy once used it; but much of the inner harbor, once naval territory, is nothing but derelict patrol boat pens and littered quaysides. We took refuge in one of the pens for the outer harbor was too exposed, safe only for the ferry, and by nightfall three other yachts had found sanctuary with us, each one tucked in its own pen. It was rather like being in some quaint boat motel. Sensing their opportunity, the port authorities collected 1,000 pesetas from each refugee in turn but nothing, other than the shelter we had found, was offered in return. But the port is attractive, backed by a massive Moorish castle, and the town behind it is a delight of small winding streets and little squares.

We made Barbate the next day by mid-afternoon. The swell was still heavy and the wind had abated, but its direction was unchanged. We were still beating. The shoals around Los Cabezos were not a pleasant sea area, but after we'd passed Cape Camarinal, yet another of the definitive Spanish capes, everything seemed to change for the better. Even the sun came out, and as we altered slightly to starboard to make directly for Barbete de Franco, we could see the long line of Cape Trafalgar on the horizon ahead. High behind Barbete, not far into the hinterland, the hill village of Vejer de la Frontera showed brilliant white in the late afternoon sun, looking almost like a magic city in a fairytale illustration. But this Spanish Oz apart, the coast between Gibraltar and Tarifa, and from Tarifa up to Cape Trafalgar, is dull and disappointing. From a distance it is not unlike the Falklands: bare hills, mountain sides rising almost directly from the coastline, bleak, windswept, and almost without a sign of human habitation. Closer to, the hills look as if they were made of rhino hide, wrinkled, dry, and grey, softened only by passing clouds and the changing light. Somewhere I read, or heard it said, that it is the least developed coastline in Europe. It may be true. Perhaps it's that wind. Barbate de Franco, fixing its port charges at a curious rate of 742 pesetas, was cheaper than Tarifa and at first sight infinitely superior; but then we realized that the harbor was filthy - was it a lack of adequate tidal cleansing? - and the washing facilities were basic. Primitive. The town itself, a longish walk away, was prosperous, bursting with rebuilding and modernity, and noise. For once, so close to our ultimate destination, we had no serious shopping to do, but the lure of sherry sold straight from the cask, the first time we had seen it on sale in this manner, ensured that we had some weight to carry back to *Terrapin* and would not lose our backpacking skills. Tom, by then overcome with the excitements of our voyaging, made serious inroads into his liters of amontillado. Going down to the galley to get one of our bottles of Mazarrón *tinta*, I suddenly realized that *Terrapin* was looking like a chicken coop after a fox had raided it. It was inexplicable. There were feathers everywhere. Soft down. Clinging feathers. As our party progressed, one by one we all took on the appearance of victims of an 18th Century mob, feathered all over, although mercifully we had not been pre-coated in tar. It was Tom's sleeping bag, an old Army bag, which somehow seemed to have worked itself behind us and under us as we sat at the saloon table, parting at the seams in the sunset of its life. So that explained the harbinger of the first curious flutter of down feathers I'd seen in Tarifa!

We sailed at 0730, a splendid red dawn behind us, and rounded the Cabo de Trafalgar, the last of our great capes, an hour later. We had decided to go to the new Puerto Sherry, just by the Puerto de Santa Maria, north of Cádiz but in the Bahia de Cádiz, and see if we could leave *Terrapin* there until early January. It was sad to be on the last stretch and even the wind didn't oblige us with a splendid last sail, but the coastline had its enchantment: the massive low lying Castillo de San Sebastian, the southern guardian fort of Cádiz, and then Cádiz itself with another fort, the Isola de Sancti Petri, and you could imagine sixteenth century history in the making. I think we cut it too close rounding the shoals to enter Cádiz Bay, but we made it and found a long line of US naval supply ships lying off Rota. There was no time to fool around looking at them, or even looking at Cádiz with its forti-fied sea walls still largely intact, for the wind had got up, it was right for us, and for the last time on this leg we let the cruising chute fly and ran up towards El Puerto de Santa Maria under a starburst blaze of white, yellow, and orange. We pulled the snuffer down only at the entrance to Puerto Sherry marina. The day's run had been 52.7 miles and *Terrapin* had covered 507.8 miles since leav-ing Santa Pola. Looked at in the light of her passage as a whole, it was not a long leg; but it might have been the one that gave us the most trouble. We were now safely out of a winter Mediterranean, through the Strait of Gibraltar, and ready to take a straight shot to the Canaries in January. Or we would be. After a little tidying up.

As ever, the tidying up took three days. We had the good fortune to find ourselves berthed alongside another cat, an early Solaris, with Jim and Alice Gibbon on board, who were wintering between Puerto Sherry and Vilamoura and would still be in Cádiz when we returned. Tom left on Day 2 to go hill walking around Medina Sidonia, still leaking feathers, his appetite for seafaring temporarily satisfied; and Phil left to take a train back to Alicante and Torrevieja early in the morning on Day 3. By then I had my air ticket from Jerez de la Frontera to London for that evening, November 13th. There was little more for me to do than note that Phil, Nikki, and I would meet on

Terrapin sometime on January 8th 1991, and we would then set about taking her to Barbados.

I went to the harbor master's office and booked a taxi to take me the airport.

NORTH ATLANTIC OCEAN
SOUTHERN SPAIN TO BARBADOS

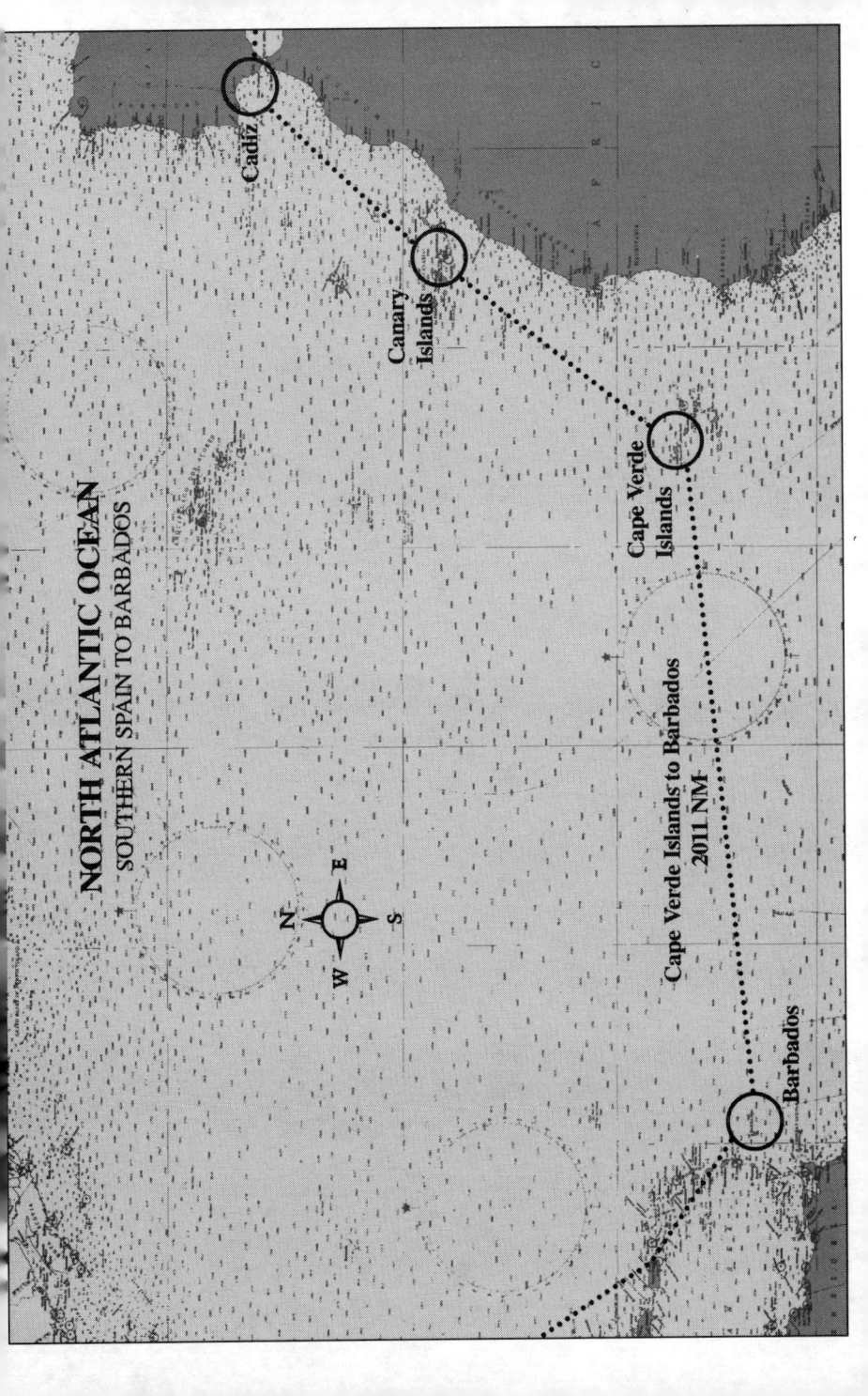

Cadiz

Canary
Islands

Cape Verde
Islands

Cape Verde Islands to Barbados
2011 NM

Barbados

N
W—E
S

BLACK WAVES

Santa Maria, Cádiz Bay, Spain, to Mogan,
Gran Canaria. January 18 - 25 1991

There are times, I think, when either the world is out
of synch or else one is totally out of synch with the world.
The great expedition didn't start well. I spent ten days in
Santa Maria before we could set out, and enjoyed little of
it. The passage itself, the first leg to the Canaries, took
seven days and I suppose we must have sailed through the
daylight hours as well as the nights, but other than our
setting out and our landfall, I have little memory of
anything but the obscurity of starless darkness, violent
motion, and a confusion of black waves and turbulent
seas.

It started well enough in Puerto Sherry. Oh, I had
the normal Day 1 chaos when everything has to be stowed
or re-stowed, and then I found that something was wrong
with my shore power hookup, which I'd never had to use
up to that point, and I had to jury rig a temporary cable
across to Jim and Alice Gibbon's Solaris. My solar
panels weren't up to keeping my batteries charged, I
didn't want to keep running my engines, for that would
have been anti-social, and I needed my SuperCool on full
time. The shore power proved such an intractable problem that I didn't get it fixed until the Virgin Islands, four
months later. The Puerto Sherry yard failed to let me
have a fax from Phil and Nikki saying that they would be
six days late, and trying to make telephone calls to
England and to the States became a waking nightmare.

The Spanish telephone system seemed designed to balk communication with the outside world rather than facilitate it, and the expense of even attempting international calls was outrageous. Day followed day. Maybe it was the weather. We were back to bitterly cold northerly winds which hit 35 knots one morning, driving rain, and 0° temperatures. All I wanted to do was get south.

Phil and Nikki arrived on the 14th, the day before the UN Deadline ordering Saddam Hussein to withdraw from Iraq, which introduced a new dimension. Do you set off on a long ocean voyage if war is imminent? What were the likely knock-on effects of full scale conflict? Santa Maria was pandemonium when we did our final provisioning. There were fuel lines at every filling station, and the supermarkets were like bear gardens as shelves were emptied in minutes. We racked up 39,317 pesetas ($408) in one store as our contribution to the doomsday mania, the panic buying, and invited Jim and Alice out to dinner. We'd leave the next day. We didn't. There was a Low over the Canaries, bad weather, and the wind was from the south. So we settled for a full trial of the inflatable, the Tinker Tramp, rigged as a life raft, and put ourselves and all our survival packs in it. I'm still not certain whether I regard the Tinker Tramp in its life raft mode as a reassuring survival fail-safe or a measure of such desperation that camping on the upturned bridge deck of a catamaran might be a better alternative. We were jammed hugger-mugger like sardines in oilskins between the flotation tubes with the inflated canopy tight above us, which could have made some aspects of personal routine interesting, but it worked. We fitted. It could be done. At midnight that night the first air strikes went in against Iraq, and a Low intensified in the North Atlantic which threatened to move our way. By the morning of the 18th another Low had materialized over Morocco and we had winds from the east at 4-5, with 7-8 in the Strait. Jim and Alice gave us a farewell present of two hot water bottles, and we sailed.

I couldn't have made a worse start, and nearly had us on the rocks within seconds. *Terrapin* has a 12V outlet on the instrument console, just underneath the port engine single lever control. I'd been fixing a hook for our 'steamer-scarer' searchlight on the bulkhead near the outlet so that the spotlight could be easy to grab at night; and I left it there, connected up, ready for use. What I hadn't realized was that the outlet should never have been set there. Any plug placed in it would prevent the engagement of reverse on the port engine, and so it proved as we left the dock. It was not an encouraging start but twenty four hours later we'd cleared Santa Maria and set a direct track from Cádiz to Santa Cruz de la Palma which had taken us immediately over two explosive dumping grounds, we'd been plagued by shipping that night in the Gibraltar convergence zone, had made 121 miles, and we were surfing along under the genny alone. The wind was still from the east, up to 20 knots or so, and it was bumpy. We'd also discovered that the house batteries were fading badly: the drain of autopilot, nav lights, instruments, and the SuperCool was too much for them. We started using an engine to charge up the batteries every few hours, first one, then the other, to keep the engine hours even. The first night hadn't been the kind of experience you wish to repeat too often, and the second and third nights were not much better. Somewhere to the north east there was the mother and father of all storms in the higher latitudes of the North Atlantic, Force 11 had been mentioned, and we were getting swells from that disturbance which were beginning to look disquietingly like mountains on the move. Even worse the swell was running in opposition to our local wind and waves. The contradiction of swell, wind, and wave built up walls of water that had *Terrapin* slithering down the slopes like a sidewinder going down a sand dune. By day it wasn't too bad. You could see the mountains coming. At night it was just too dark to see anything, and your first warning was the hissing rush of a breaking wave crest as a great black wall of water reared up at the stern and then broke under the boat with a roar like a train going through a tunnel. We took some water side-on into the cockpit, which wasn't in the fun spec for a centre cockpit boat, and on Night 3 we were pooped at about two in the morning. Suddenly, in all the noise and the blackness, I was soaked by a roaring tidal bore that swept over the aft coachroof, there was white water everywhere, the cockpit had become a swimming pool, and Phil and Nikki, who were off watch, surfaced as if the final bell had sounded. *Terrapin* shook herself, the cockpit drained, and we sailed on. In Iraq the air war continued.

By Day 4 it was better and we even had the cruising chute in use; then the wind fell to barely 2 knots although the sea state remained. By the middle of Night 6 we had about 175 miles to run and we seemed to be drawn inexorably closer and closer to the Selvagen Islands, a nasty series of shipwreckers lying well offshore, but right on track to the Canary Islands. I'd set our course aiming to pass far away from them, but by *force majeure* or wind and current we sighted the Selvagen Grande light which was almost too close for comfort, and then saw the real horror of the island chain as dawn broke. I don't think we needed a reminder about the frailty of craft at sea but later that day the weather became impossible. La Palma, the westernmost of the Canaries, was out of the question. We altered for Mogon in Gran Canaria, just over a hundred miles away. It didn't matter, in truth, where we went as long as we could rest and provision, and we were there by 1600 the next day. We took the final run-in slowly, well-reefed as a precaution against the notorious Canary wind acceleration zones, where winds, tunnelled between the volcanic, moonscape islands, can redouble their strength and lay you flat in seconds.

How had we done? Seven days at sea. 760.53 nm. On the face of it, not at all badly. But we had problems. The electrics were a real curse. I had hoped our solar panels would keep the house batteries topped up, but it seemed it was not to be. The power drainers were undoubtedly the Autohelm 4000, the SuperCool, and the nav lights. Although we had hand steered on occasion, it was unthinkable to do without the autopilot. Watchkeeping would have become a tyranny, and our whole crew schedule, as well as navigation time, mainte-nance time, cooking time, relaxation, and rest, would have been knocked out of the realms of sensible manage-ment into a grim endurance test. I don't think we could have given up the SuperCool. It wasn't sodas and cold beer, it was vital perishables that required a 36°F setting to prolong their life. As for the nav lights, we were still in a high traffic density area of the ocean. We had a close call with an overtaking ship our last night at sea, as we approached Gran Canaria. Perhaps later, in the open ocean, we could forget the nav lights. Not now. No way. There was only one way to solve it and that was to go for another generator, either wind or water. That much was patently clear.

Another problem had become patently clear. We had crew trouble. Somewhere along the line the magic had vanished and Phil, Nikki, and I were veering into a fairly fundamental state of total incompatibility. Why? It's easy to speculate but hard to be specific, for human relationships, even on land, can be so tenuous, so mercurial, that if you start with a triangle, add in the small boat factor, a bumpy ride over a chunk of ocean, and an enterprise that none of the three had undertaken before, the milk and honey may run thin. If you were to ask me now what I reckon is the single most important factor in the business of taking a small boat to sea, I'd say (given, it almost goes without saying, a well-found boat) it is choice of crew. Every time. You must have total compatibility. It's vital. It's also something you can't predict: it may develop, it will happen if you are fortunate. And once you have found it, to paraphrase the lyrics of *South Pacific*, 'never let it go'. At risk of worrying at the subject like a terrier with a bone, I would go on. Phil and I had sailed together from Torrevieja to Cádiz happily enough. A male on male is perhaps the easiest of all relationships to sustain, more so if you have a bonding common interest. When Phil and Nikki joined *Terrapin* together, in effect a two-people team had left their own twin boat for another, run by someone Phil had only known briefly and Nikki didn't know at all. Perhaps part of it was the old saw, different ships, different splices. How would it have been if I'd crewed for them? All I do know is that somewhere in the weave of the half-hundred threads and the thousand-and-one complications in the pattern of human relationships, something went wrong. And I know that I was inadequate to cope with it: I was too stressed out, too taken up in my learning curve, and in the management of the whole enterprise, to look around me until it was too late, to relax and take five minutes off and take stock of where we were, rather than where we were going.

We were in Mogan longer than I expected. In my original plan, time in the Canaries was to have been a 3-4 day rest and maintenance period with a 500 hour engine service thrown in. No more than that. But there was the generator business, and determined to cure the problem, I ordered an Ampair wind/water turbine to be air freighted in from England. We'd arrived late on a Friday afternoon, and when I spoke to the makers the next day, there seemed no reason why it wouldn't be in Gran Canaria by Tuesday. They promised that it would be delivered to the air freight handlers at London's Heathrow Airport by early Monday morning. We could fit the generator on the Tuesday and sail on Wednesday. Ampair kept their promise. By Monday the generator was delivered to Heathrow and promptly locked into an air freight quarantine compound for 48 hours. At the time neither we, nor indeed the Mogan agent, had any idea that the Gulf War had resulted in a mandatory embargo on the movement of any air freight until it had been quarantined for 48 hours in case it contained time charges. The missing generator, eventually traced without undue difficulty, reached Madrid on Friday and to their credit, Iberia got it on to Las Palmas de Gran Canaria the next day. But that was a Saturday. It was Monday February 4th before we were able to claim it.

So we slipped *Terrapin* briefly to scrub her hulls, and cleaned her from masthead to keel, slowly restoring our relationship, though the tension was there, it was still unpleasant. It's not what you need when if you want to start listing your real concerns, you should go out and buy a larger notebook. But by then I'd beaten the Spanish telephone system, or at last mastered it, and I spoke to Victoria in London almost daily. Janet, in Vermont, was still on another planet. "Go for it, Boo" she said when I spoke of calling it off. "Don't be silly. Give it time. As it is, you hardly see each other at sea. You're alone on your watches for most of the time. Just go for it"

Wise girl. We fitted the generator on the Tuesday and sailed the next day, which was Wednesday, February 6th.

ISLANDS OF NO RETURN

Mogan, Gran Canaria, to Porto Grande, São
Vicente, Cape Verde Islands. February 6 - 13 1991

There's nothing in the way as you head from Gran
Canaria south to São Vicente in the Cape Verde Islands.
No Selvagen Islands, nothing nasty like that. You can set
a course of 230° M and hold it until you make your
landfall, 831 miles away. Perhaps the wind may take you
slightly west of your intended track, but the Canary
current is with you all the way, forming, with the wind,
one of the world's great ocean conveyor belts. You are
running safely some 200 miles off the Mauritanian coast
with two miles of water under your keel, keels in our case,
all the time. This must be the leg, we said, where an
Atlantic crossing becomes the dream Trade Wind passage: deep ultramarine blue water, clear skies with little
cotton ball clouds, and flying fish, garnered from the
deck each morning, fried in canned New Zealand butter
for breakfast.

It came close, but it wasn't quite like that. For a start
the Trade Winds weren't there, but the wind was north
easterly all the time, between 5-10 knots. It's tempting
fate to complain of light winds, but although the direction
was good, it wasn't quite strong enough. The common
doctrine, in the tactics school of trans-Atlantic crossings,
is to head south east from the Canary Islands in a gentle
parabolic curve, and know that you will pick up the Trade
Winds sooner or later, wherever their northernmost limit

may be at that time. The traditional pickup point is reckoned to be 25°N 25°W or 100 miles NW of the Cape Verde Islands. Somewhere around there. So why go all the way down to the islands themselves? Porto Grande harbor is described in one Pilot book as "amongst the finest in the eastern Atlantic, giving total protection from northwest through east to south, and partial protection from south around to west . . . usually millpond calm". The same source, dispelling the attraction of a perfect haven, goes on to add "but as yet there are no shoreside facilities of any kind, not even a secure or convenient dinghy landing". And so you think about it, and wonder if the Cape Verdes, at 16°N, are not just too far south and too far out of the way.

Weather was one reason for going all the way south to the islands. That year the higher latitudes of the North Atlantic were a cauldron of violent storms, and the hurricane that had plagued us distantly when we set out from Cádiz had moved from the north west of Ireland to the Bay of Biscay. Foul northern weather, heavy swells, and high seas were shattering traditional Trade Wind patterns well south of the Tropic of Cancer. Get south, get south was the only answer.

My second reason was a painting. Years back, shortly after we were married, Janet and I had found a painting, an oil on a single heavy oak board with a faded gold frame, virtually abandoned in the junk corridor of a small East Kent antique shop. It was a marine painting of four British 24 gun frigates of the Red Squadron entering a harbor, which might have been Mediterranean. The background hills were volcanic and their shape very definite, unmistakable: if you could find the matching skyline. The size and shape of the port was little use in identification, for much must have changed over 150 or 250 years. The painting could be dated by its subject to 1725-1864: the first date marked the introduction of the 'standard' 24 gun frigate, and 1864 was the date of the abolition of the three squadron, Red, White, and Blue, organization. I went to the National Maritime Museum at Greenwich. They were fascinated, but couldn't identify the location. Years later, doing research on Easter Island for a lecture, I read Katherine Scoresby Routledge's book *Mana* on her epic 1914 expedition to Easter Island. The expedition itself was an extraordinary example of a philanthropic search for enlightenment in the 19th Century aristocratic pattern, for it was mounted entirely at their expense in their own yacht, which had been specially built for it. There, amongst the illustrations, was her drawing of "Porto Grande, St Vincent, Cape Verde Islands." I looked at our painting. That was it. My skyline was slightly displaced, or it was evident that my artist was just rounding the first headland, but it looked right. It could be it. I had to go there.

But these were not the only reasons. There was a more fundamental one. Esoteric, if you like. I mentioned "the world's great ocean conveyor belts." I have a fixation that the first civilizations spread in prehistoric times from the Middle East across the Mediterranean; and that wind and current eventually took the early merchant navigators, the Phoenician carriers of Egyptian and Minoan culture and skills, across the Atlantic to Central America, by way of the Canaries and the Cape

Verde Islands. This thesis has been discounted time and time again in their wisdom by conventional academics, who dismiss the theory as untenable due to a lack of hard evidence. Die-hard *diffusionists* disagree. There are far too many similarities in the major prehistoric civilizations to dismiss them as random coincidence. Everything points to a diffusion of civilization from a common source over a considerable period of time, during which, very obviously, the receiving peoples must have modified or distorted their inheritance so that over the centuries the nature of their beliefs and the form of their culture took on unique characteristics. What hard evidence do you expect to find after five thousand years? The more I've travelled, the more convinced I've become that Thor Heyerdahl was right when he suggested that Easter Island and the Marquesas were settled from South America; and of course those Olmec negroid heads in Tabasco had their origin in Nubian Egypt, and surely the stonework the Incas inherited had its ancient origins in the Nile Valley? I'm sure much of what we've been taught in school is incomplete, far too shallow, too recent. We've been seduced by the mythology of the Colombian legend; far from being the first, he was a late comer on the American scene. The very elements that dictate your optimum course on a sailboat, prevailing winds and ocean currents, are the arteries of civilization that have girdled the world as surely as a moving walkway since Man first clung to a floating log. So, let's follow this through. If this is your conviction, why not set out to see how it feels? If, IF deliberate Trans-Atlantic voyaging did take place 2,000 years before Columbus, the Mediterranean seafarers could have made it only one way, with the Canary Current and the Trade Winds. The Phoenicians and later the Romans, who reached the Americas too late in their history to have the drive to exploit their discoveries, must have staged in the Canaries and the Cape Verde Islands long before the Portuguese discovered them. And if you believe it, why not go that way? In a small craft? Try it for size.

It took us eight days to reach São Vicente. None of it was remarkable sailing for, as I've said, the winds were light. Our progress owed more to the cruising chute and twin engines than it did to full sails, and at one time our speed fell to little more than 3 knots. There was no stress and certainly no Trades, but it was pleasant enough with day time temperatures around 75°F. We streamed the water turbine and for the first time our battery problems were over, but it was hardly a valid test of the Ampair system for we were motor sailing for part of the time almost every day. On Day 4 dolphins joined us, talking to each other as they crisscrossed and leapt ahead of our twin hulls, their dorsal fins within inches of our feet as we sat above them on the forward edge of the bridgedeck. We read and sunbathed by day, identified the stars by night, fixed a slipping autohelm belt, and replaced the masthead tricolor bulb, which failed surprisingly early in its life. The first flying fish landed in the cockpit when I was on watch one night and I put it in a bucket of sea water to show Phil and Nikki, and then took pity on it and returned it to its element. The next night something black flew across the periphery of my vision as I was sitting against the cockpit coaming, hit me straight on the ear, failed to penetrate and fell into my lap. It was sharp snouted, wet and slithery. Another flying fish. Phil wouldn't believe it. The night after it happened to him. I can't think why the flying fish of the Cape Verde Plateau should have this homing instinct for human ears. If it had happened again, we might have become seriously disturbed; but we were left to run in to the islands in peace.

The peace ended in the last two days as we started to sight ships, and by 0700 on Day 8 we had our landfall. By early that afternoon we had something like two hours to run when the head strop of the cruising chute parted, the sail, secured only by the tack and the clew, flew out instantly over the bows and collapsed. Within seconds we'd run over it. As ill-luck had it, the port engine was running at that time to top up the batteries for we'd handed the water turbine some hours before. It was clear that we had an unholy tangle under *Terrapin* and I stripped to dive and clear it. There's something funny about swimming in the deep ocean. I can't explain why it should be different swimming with two miles of water under your feet rather than more conventional 'out-of-your-depth' depths, but it is. There's something fundamentally psychological, something unnerving about it. The weather was worsening and the sea state was building up while I was in the water, but it wasn't that, and it wasn't the fear of sharks, although I kept doing 360° checks for dark shapes and had Phil watching for fins. The cruising chute was badly damaged, wrapped round the port propeller and I had to cut it loose. We got under way again under the genoa and sailed into the channel between Santo Antão and São Vicente to find ourselves in a wind acceleration zone and 'tide rip' that would count as a world class suicide run for board sailers, shot past the jagged Ilheu dos Passaros crowned with its extraordinary fortification, the wind was Force 7 by then, and anchored in Porto Grande at 1630. There was no sign of anyone around. No immigration. No customs. Just four other yachts, well-spaced, and the north east wind, gusting up to Force 8 over the anchorage rated to be "amongst the finest in the eastern Atlantic, giving total protection from northwest through east to south . . .".

We spent four days there, anchored in 10ft of water with 20ft of 5/16th chain and 60ft of nylon out to a 25lb CQR, and our 25lb Studland with 20ft of chain set in line with the main anchor. The wind never died. It reduced to average 20-25 knots, but higher gusts were not uncommon and we hit 7s again, if not 8s. Our fenders, slung outboard to free deck space, were blown aft at 45° most of the time, and an inflatable in those conditions was as stable as a tin tray on ice, but at least there was no fetch. Just wavelets. This unremitting terrible wind never left us in peace, even at night, for it howled like abanshee as it passed through the rigging. It seemed clear to me that we had reached a kind of Ultima Thule. These islands were the end of the known world. Places of No Return. Once you were in the Cape Verde Islands (I'm talking now of those of us in sailboats) there was no way in which you could turn back, return north to the Mediterranean. And once you set out again, you would have to go on. Either go on south to the Cape of Good Hope, or set out across the Atlantic. There could be no turning back, other than by taking the full North Atlantic circle, swinging north with the Gulf Stream to pick up the Westerlies, and so, eventually, make it back to Northern Europe.

Two days after our arrival there were seven of us there in São Vicente. Two German yachts, *Lady M* (who had been with us in Mogon), and *Donnerkiel II*. There were two French, who kept themselves far apart, one Swede, and a Swiss boat. We refilled our water tanks, ferrying 2 gallon can by 2 gallon can, and refilled our diesel tanks by much the same method. The Pilot was right. There were no shoreside facilities, not even a secure or convenient dinghy landing, but in any event food provisioning was out of the question. There was nothing to buy, even in the fish market, where the entire catch one day was nothing but two octopi and we arrived to find a very large woman in a faded floral shift beating the two unfortunate cephalopods to death, flailing one, and then the other, against the rough concrete floor. Leaving the death scene we had some success in our searching for we found a cobbler with a treadmill sewing machine who volunteered to remake our cruising chute. His shop was too small to spread 550 square feet of sail, so with his consent we moved his sewing machine out into the street. There he set himself up happily enough, surrounded by a small horde of curious children, and while we held the chute down in the gusts of wind, he cut and remade the sail. It was worth trying. In truth it failed. It never set properly.

We were waiting for the weather. That something was bad outside in the wider Atlantic was evident to all of us in the marooned group of seven, but there seemed no way of getting any kind of reliable report in São

Vicente. There was officialdom there, in Mindelo, we'd cleared entry formalities the day after we'd arrived and had been received well, but nothing was geared to our kind of peripatetic life. Certainly no routine weather forecasts. Late on the second day on a long walk round the commercial harbor I found a Russian freighter, the *Paulik Lazishkin*, and invited myself on board. That day we had our first weatherfax and a date to join up for dinner ashore. What of the weather? Apparently it was bad with a worsening situation to the north, 15ft waves and high winds. So we joined up for dinner that night, and the next, and did our drinking in a bar festooned with Chinese paper lanterns. The old basic commonality of human communication came into play. German, Russian, English, Portuguese, island native, none of us on the face of it had a tongue in common and yet we spoke and exchanged an astonishing amount of information. If, you were bound to think, if everyone, regardless of nation, were thrown together into a melting pot as children, would not one universal language emerge within two generations? Would that help make it a better world? The Russians gave me a souvenir note at the end of our visit. It read (sic):

> "From members of crew m.v. Paulik Lazishkin to master of yacht Terrapin. With better wishes and good luck on islands Cape Verde. I would like you to remember following. Nobody knows what will be tomorrow and the three things most difficult are: to keep a secret, to forget an injanery and to make good use of free time.

Our address: [and the address followed in Cyrillic script]".

The weatherfaxes, almost impossible to read, indicated the worst was over. We had to get going. We were halfway through February and I had a date to meet Janet in Barbados at the start of March. But it wasn't that alone, for that kind of compulsion is the worst of all reasons for setting out to sea. We had to move on because there was nothing more to do in the Cape Verde Islands. I'd failed to decide whether my painting had Porto Grande and Mindelo as its background: it was just possible, but I think not, and even now I'm not certain. Perhaps the most cogent reason for moving on was that we had nothing to offer these people, who themselves had nothing at all. The Canary Islands, at first sight, are a barren desolation but Spanish subsidies, tourist dollars, and the produce of sheltered inland valleys have given the islands a viable economy. The Cape Verde Islands have lost it all the way down the line. The land is windswept and bare. Water is scarce. Nothing grows there. They are on the way to nowhere, no longer a staging post. There is no possibility that any part of them could ever serve any useful function as a tourist resort. Small wonder Portugal slipped them into independence with little hesitation. What of the future? God knows. God only knows.

Rafael Ramos Fortes ('Raf') and Armando Dias Fortes ('Duca'), I share your concern. Both boys, who had adopted us from the moment we first set foot on the beach at Mindelo, became our friends while we were there.

TRANS-ATLANTIC

São Vicente, Cape Verde Islands, to Bridgetown,
Barbados. February 17 - March 7 1991

Lady M left for Brazil on the afternoon of the 17th
and we left Porto Grande, about an hour later, at 1630,
under engines. The late departure was due to no particu-
lar reason. A change from setting out in the early
morning, if you like, for change's sake or recognition that
there was no way, with 2,000 miles of open ocean to run,
we could predict our landfall off Barbados; so it hardly
mattered when we started. Fifteen minutes later we
passed the Ilheu dos Passaros and it was gusting 7,
increasing in strength. In the channel between the two
islands, the Canal de São Vicente, the seas were awesome
(not a word I use lightly) and the wind was well into Force
8. We were making 6 knots under the staysail alone, a 32
sq. ft pocket handkerchief, and the following seas were
sweeping us on as if we were caught in some nightmare
theme park with an unstoppable, maniacal mega-wave
machine. If we'd wanted to divert, or to turn back, it
would have been impossible. To broach would have been
disaster, to try to alter course out of the centre channel
would have risked being smashed on the rocks. By 2130
the mad race was over and we were in the wind shadow
of Santo Antão, although the sea state was still high. Two
hours later our boat speed had dropped to 0 and we were
wallowing. We started the starboard engine.

It was not the most promising of all starts, more so
to a much-dreamt-of Trade Wind passage, but I don't

know what I might, reasonably, have expected without fantasizing or deluding myself. The next day was little improvement, if we're still chasing those images of cotton ball clouds and the gentle force of constant benign Trades. My log entry put it the way it was:

"Sloppy broken seas with heavy swell from NE. Wind 11-14 knots. Overcast. Light rain at times. Started clearing 1100. Some sun at midday but progressively worse in terms of sea state during day. Heavy confused swell. Horrid. Sky 7/8ths [cloud cover] and looking heavy. Only good thing wind relatively constant and boat speed OK - could be better, but achieved 110.22 in first 24 hrs. at sea."

We were averaging 4.5 knots which was, in truth, less than I'd hoped. What can you expect? Another knot would have been great, two knots would have been the heart's desire. So much depends on the sea state, and wallowing around virtually stationary in the middle of the night hadn't helped. We never achieved a sensational day's run. Our best was 134.59 and for most of the time we had to be content with a fairly steady progress at around 5 knots. Disappointing for a catamaran? Perhaps a touch slower than the popular image would suggest, but remember we were heavily laden at the start: eighty gallons of water, 37 gallons of diesel, and enough food to keep us alive for thirty six days without touching survival packs. And remember too that *Terrapin* was no racer, just a small, deep-bellied, blue water cruising cat. She was, to continue the analysis, a patient, dogged, forgiving boat, for whose sea-keeping qualities, by then, I was beginning to have a higher and higher regard. We made it to Barbados in seventeen and a half days, which can't have been too bad, can it?

So what about this trans-Atlantic crossing business? You draw a track on the Atlantic chart and for the first time you're working off a chart which shows more ocean than land. That thin pencil line, running 283°M from the southern tip of Santo Antão to Barbados, seems to run forever with no reference at all, so to give it some comprehensible, achievable definition you put in the half way point. The faint cross, lost somewhere north of the Vema Fracture Zone, is not enough. By then you're noting every feature of the ocean floor for there's nothing else to tell you where you are, or where you're going. So you subdivide the distance, so that you'll pass one of your markers every 3-4 days. That's good for morale. Then you settle down to your passage. Routine is everything, a gentle, relaxed routine which gives each person no less than eight consecutive hours off-watch, and allows the whole crew to come together once a day over supper each evening, without anyone paying the penalty of losing out on sleep time. I've read every sailing book I can get my hands on and I've tried, by now, every variant in the watchkeeping routine. It's the kind of subject which always seems to arouse controversy or certainly strong convictions, for everyone has their own approach, but I'm convinced that four hour watches are the founding base of the perfect system. Of course in foul conditions, in high stress situations, you fit what you're doing to the day, but I'm talking now about passage making. Four hour watches work well for a crew of three, and allow someone to concentrate on cooking if you have a crew of four. As far as sleep is concerned, I'm certain that unless you get four hours unbroken sleep as a minimum, your mental and physical condition deteriorates significantly. We've all stretched and pushed ourselves in emergencies, sometimes for far too long, and survived. But it's culpable idiocy to become tired at sea. As my Russian said "nobody knows what will be tomorrow". Do you keep altering the watch schedule, so that you all rotate through the 24 hour cycle? I think not. The human body responds best to a set rhythm, even if your periods of work and sleep are at variance with the natural Circadian rhythm. The vital thing is that you get that sleep: and can, if necessary, sleep not just for four hours without being woken up, but six or seven, if you wish. Again, with a crew of three, if someone is responsible for navigation, and someone has the responsibility for the main meal of the day, the watchkeeping pattern settles naturally enough to give each person the right periods of the day off-watch to attend to their special tasks without impinging on their rest. At the end of the day, if it seems that rotation is only fair, that everyone should experience the orange flame of dawn and the diamonds and black velvet of the best of the night sky, change the pattern once a week but not more often than that. Remember you are programming complex vertebrates, not a set of sailing instruments.

Does boredom set in? I don't think so. With routine maintenance, navigation, cooking, fishing, sunbathing, listening to the World News, music, and talking, you soon find that you're short of time for reading and the pile of books you brought with you, the ones you'd always promised yourself you'd read at sea, are lying unopened.

What are the fears? No more than the four standard fears of putting out to sea. The first is the fear of losing someone overboard. There's only one answer to that: make it impossible. We wore harness on deck all the time, clipped on before moving into the cockpit from below, and we stayed clipped on in the cockpit. We rigged jacklines so that wherever you moved, you were tied to the boat. There is no other way. Yes, we had all the standard Man Overboard equipment, but there were many times when, if one of us had fallen overboard or had been swept into the ocean, it would have been certain death; and, this apart, the probability of carrying out a successful rescue in mid-ocean most of the time is not high, even if, in the middle of the night, you realized that someone was missing. The other fears? Being run down is No 2. Hitting something is Fear 3. If someone's on watch the whole time, you shouldn't be run down but it's amazing how, in the blackness of a foul night, you can come uncomfortably close to it. A radar alarm helps but not all ships operate their radar on the high seas, just as you soon learn that few ships keep a 24 hour radio watch. You're on your own. Take it that no-one's looking out for you or gives a damn whether there just might be a little sailboat in their way. You have to look out for them, and you take the evasive action. The Rules of the Road are the kind of game you play in coastal sailing, if indeed then. What about hitting something? The container washed off a ship and floating just under the surface is everyone's dread. There are enough of them about, but statistical probability is on your side for there's a lot of ocean out there. Narrow waters and choke points may well alter the odds, but in the open ocean all you can do is hope that you won't hit something, and that if you do, your boat's construction, positive flotation, and your own damage control skills will save the day. Think it through: what if ...?

It leaves heavy weather as the one remaining fear. I don't think I've met anyone who doesn't have a latent, lurking fear that they might get caught in unexpected bad weather each time they sail. On short passages the answer is plan so that you can avoid it, but once you are committed to an ocean crossing, the die is cast. You just hope that the pilot charts are right, that the statistical probability of storms at that time of year in that part of the ocean really is zero. You know, deep down, that this may well have been the way it was in the past; but now? But now?

We were alone on the ocean, far away from the shipping lanes, and we saw no ships. Then in the middle of the night after we'd been at sea for four days we suddenly found ourselves on a collision course with a large ship which appeared to be lying motionless, without lights, right across our path. Our radar alarm was on, but hadn't sounded. We called the unknown ship on VHF, and on single sideband. No answer. So we started our engines, put the steamer-scarer on our sails, blinding white light, and our night vision went out of the window. At that moment she came to life, there were lights on her mast, a red over white over red, and she turned north and slowly moved away. An hour later she was over the horizon. Eleven days were to pass before we saw another ship. These were the only two ships we saw during the crossing.

You could say happiness is a trans-Atlantic passage with nothing exciting in it, one in which petty concerns and small comforts are the staple issues of each day. Nikki got the comforts right, baking fresh bread each day which I'd never expected. I didn't think that we'd be reduced to Magellan's living conditions ". . . we remained another three months and twenty days without taking in provisions or other refreshments, and we ate only old biscuit reduced to powder and full of grubs, and stinking from the dirt which rats had made on it . . .", but the difference Nikki's administration made was significant. I wish I could say the same for my fishing. Day after day I could only conclude that the Atlantic Ocean was fished out. Finished. Nothing left. Then one morning the reel screamed against the pawl as the line ran out forever, as if we'd hooked the ocean floor. It took me 55 minutes to land the fish, and I thought I'd never make it, more so in the final round when the vast, powerful, lunging torpedo shape at the end of the line seemed far from ready to quit, astonishingly strong. If we'd both been in the water, the fish would have won. Phil with superhuman strength swung the fish into the cockpit with the gaff, Nikki screamed and disappeared, and the two of us were left sharing our narrow space with an angry five foot King Mackerel. When it was still, I tried to lift it and could hardly hold the fish at shoulder level. It must have weighed over 35 lbs. The bloody, guilt-inducing process of cleaning and cutting it up took me three hours, and for three days we ate nothing but mackerel cooked in a thousand ways, which can pall. With infinite regret much of our fish went to feed the sharks, and as if Nature censured our prodigal waste, we caught nothing else. The rest of our daily concerns were dull fare. Replacing the autohelm drive belt, which proved our emergency steering arrangement was useless, had us wallowing for over an hour while we learned how to do it. Adding to the list of failures, despite the best efforts of the Mindelo cobbler the cruising chute, as I said earlier, proved hopelessly asymmetrical, and we lost the bitter end of its halyard to the masthead. It hardly mattered by then, but I tried to recover it. Despite our mast steps and my harness with its two karabiners, I failed, and I never made it past the radar reflector just above the cross trees, scared to death by the whiplash motion up there.

What about successes? Every day we were going forward, getting there. Noon day cross followed noon day cross on the chart and that thin pencil line was no longer intimidating but became a ladder laid across the ocean. Every few days we changed time zones, slowly reinforcing our proximity to Western Atlantic Time, and I started calling Janet in Vermont on the radio, confirming our date to meet in Barbados at the end of the first week in March. Even the weather was improving:

"Perhaps the best 'Trade Wind' day yet. Deep blue ocean, no clouds, fair breeze, sea state perhaps a little too broken yet but tolerable. Washing and showers! First time possible. Fishing - but no fish."

That was Day 14. In the meantime the Gulf War was over, ended by the attrition of remorseless bombing as well as by a strategic outflanking that owed its success to the very navigation system we were using, GPS. For the first time a desert war had been fought using satellite rather than celestial navigation, and the war colleges of the world could start to amend their text books. For the yachtsman (I dislike the term, but use it to describe the non-military user) GPS was at its peak then, for the Pentagon had no option but to turn off the degrading 'Selective Availability' which, in their view, prevented enemies of the United States from using GPS to pop their missiles into the mouths of American silos. To give GPS to every ground unit in the Gulf Force, the Pentagon's panic buy had cleared the stocks of every marine supplier in the US (as well as Magellan's shelves, then the world leader in hand held sets), and none of these instruments, intended for the commercial market, could work through Selective Availability. The Pentagon switched off SA. Not only was GPS cover continuous, but its accuracy was superb. It was reassuring, but it was no surprise when at 2130 on the night of March 6th the loom of the lights of Barbados came up on the starboard bow. At 0600 the next morning I called asking for permission to enter Deep Water Harbor, and one hour later we were secured, dwarfed by four cruise ships.

It was no big deal, you could say, not with GPS. I'd agree. What about the first Atlantic sailers, the Phoenicians? Let's accept that the first voyages must have been accidental drift voyages, but someone, sometime, made it back. Remember, even then they knew that the world was round, they had fixed the value of a degree, and predicted the circumference of the earth with no more than a 10% error. Their star path navigation was better than our celestial navigation in the 18th Century. How good was it? Who can tell? Let's guess that it was accurate to somewhere between 30-60 miles. On the face of it, that margin of error could take you past your destination, particularly if the stars were obscured, and that leads us directly to the importance of the Canary Islands and the Cape Verde Islands to the prehistoric sailor. Not only were they staging posts on that moving beltway of wind and current, but archipelagic islands offer a safety net. You can pick up the peak of a volcanic island at something like eighty miles, but let's say it's thirty miles. If you draw rings with 30 mile radii around each of the Canary Islands, and each of the Cape Verde Islands, you have two infallible safety nets, stretched across something like 300 miles of ocean in each case. Wind and current alone will drop you within that net. You can then make the final adjustments to achieve your desired landfall. As for the western Atlantic, you have the whole chain of the Lesser and Greater Antilles and the Bahamas as your catchment, but if you missed every island, you would still make Brazil, Central America, or North America, just as surely as going back with the west winds, you could not miss Europe.

I would, quite happily, have done my crossing without GPS. In the early days, when we left the Cape Verde Islands, I was convinced that our painstaking navigation was, in truth, totally unnecessary. We could, I'm sure, have done no more than make sure that the sun was rising behind us each morning and setting over our bows each evening, and only started to pay attention to our navigation when we had two hundred miles to run.

The 'conveyor belt' was that certain. We know that by 2500 BC the Egyptians had ships well over 100 ft in length. By 150 BC maritime technology had leapt forward, as you would expect, after a further two thousand years of experience, and by then three masted merchant ships, carrying two sails on their main masts, had a cargo capacity of 300-1900 tons. Two hundred years later we're talking about ships with an LOA of 180 ft, a 45 ft beam, and a hull depth of 44 ft, capable of carrying 1200 tons or 600 passengers. The 'standard' merchant ship of the day would have made Columbus's *Santa Maria* look like a river barge, and *Santa Maria* was 50 ft longer than *Terrapin*. In fact *Santa Maria*'s beam was the exact equal of *Terrapin*'s length. What am I trying to say? Simply that the Phoenician captain had a craft with better sea keeping qualities than *Santa Maria*, or *Terrapin* come to that, certainly a vessel more than six times the size of *Terrapin*, and a daily run of 120 nm was well within their reach: in other words, a seventeen day crossing from the Cape Verde Islands to a landfall in the Antilles.

Why didn't I just forget the GPS and play it their way? Only because I had a date. To meet Janet. And she was waiting in Bridgetown, Barbados, with a bottle of champagne on ice.

NORTH AMERICA AND THE CARIBBEAN
BARBADOS TO JUPITER, FLORIDA.

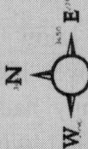

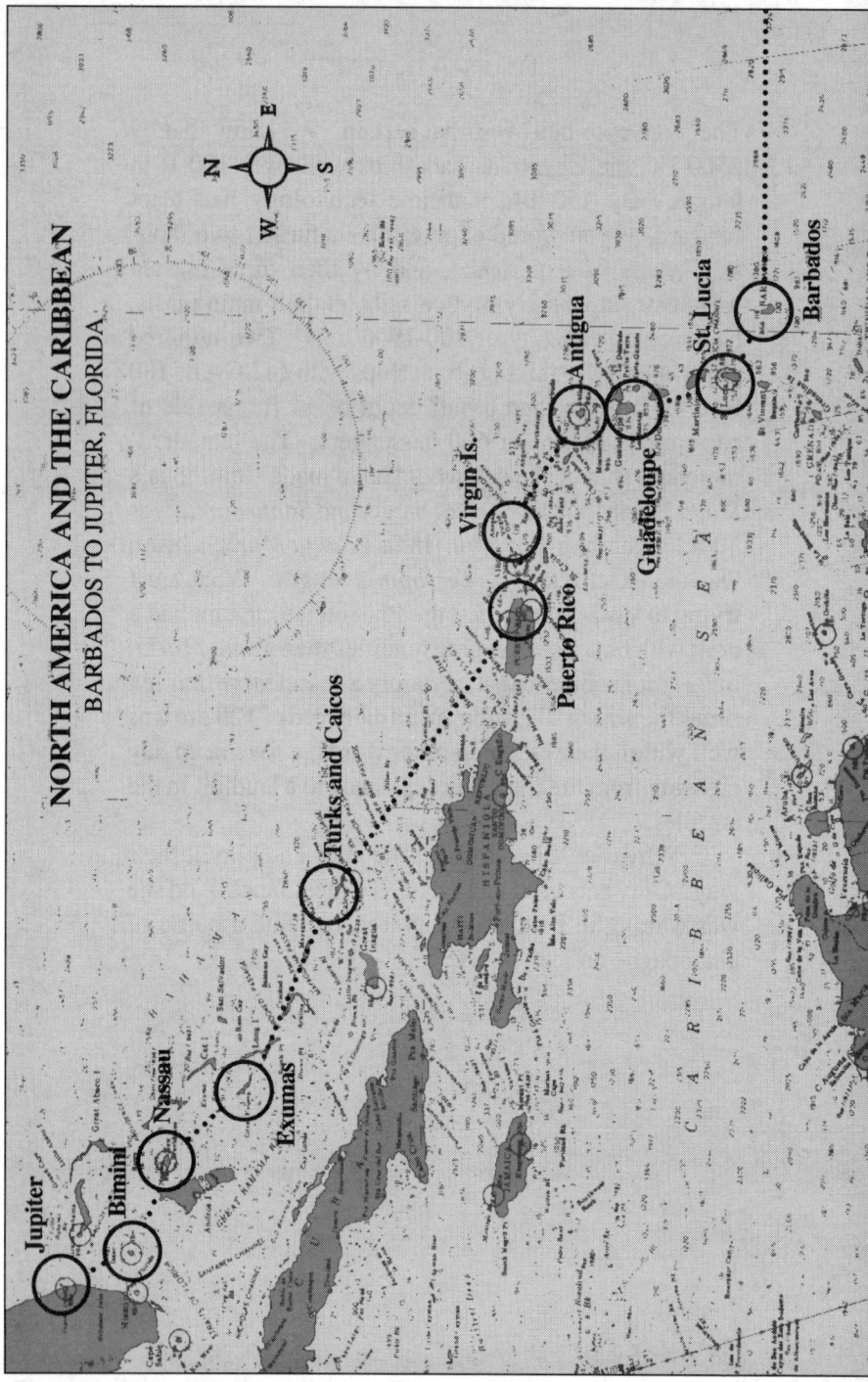

Jupiter

Bimini

Nassau

Exumas

Turks and Caicos

Virgin Is.

Puerto Rico

Guadeloupe

Antigua

St. Lucia

Barbados

C A R I B B E A N   S E A

CRUISING IN PARADISE

Bridgetown, Barbados, to Virgin Gorda,
British Virgin Islands. March 11 - April 17 1991

I like Barbados. I'd been there before, years back,
and I've been there again since my trans-Atlantic passage, but I chose the wrong place for my landfall. Why
did I choose it? Not because it's the most easterly of the
Caribbean islands, the closest to Africa. There's nothing
but eighty miles in that, which is neither here nor there
when you're thinking of weeks at sea. Barbados fell into
place because I wanted to start at the south of the Antilles
chain and work my way north, island hopping to Puerto
Rico, and then to the Turks and Caicos Islands, the
Bahamas, and on to Florida. I didn't want to start in
Trinidad or Tobago, for I'd lived there as a boy over two
years and the Gulf of Paria held little attraction as an
initial cruising ground. The Grenadines, you'll say at
once, should have been my choice: but I crossed them off
my list. I'd no idea what kind of shape *Terrapin* might
be in after her trans-Atlantic, and I thought I might need
more sophisticated backup facilities than Grenada, St
Vincent, or anywhere in the Grenadines could offer.
Barbados would have everything. I got it wrong.

There's nowhere satisfactory to anchor in Barbados and nowhere you can tie up alongside in safety and
comfort. Deep Water Harbor is reserved for cruise ships
and commercial traffic, and your options are limited to
two less than attractive alternatives. You can anchor off
in Carlisle Bay, which is rolly to say the least, as Atlantic

swells and waves swing round Needham's Point and your dinghy trips ashore are going to be surf landings every time; or you can tie up alongside The Wharf in the Careenage in the heart of Bridgetown. We did that, and never felt at ease there. The same surge that put us off Carlisle Bay gives you no rest, the so-called marina at the end of the Careenage is overcrowded, and you can't work your way into a better position or secure yourself by taking a line off at all four corners. There simply isn't the space. Maybe *Terrapin* and I had claustrophobia after the open ocean, but there were too many people around Bridgetown. It wasn't the natives who caused the angst so much as the thousands disgorged from the towering white hulls in the Deep Water Harbor. You see the look of disdain on the faces of the Bajan shop assistants in the Broad Street stores, and it reinforces your culture shock at re-exposure to your own kind as tourist figures ill-suited to the near-nudity of halter tops, bikini bras, bare midriffs, and abbreviated shorts fall like locusts on the Duty Free goods.

Janet and I offered Phil and Nikki a chance to sail on with us and see something of the Caribbean, but the pull of their own lives dominated and after two days they flew to London. We'd had long enough to talk about what we'd all do when we reached Barbados and their decision came as no surprise, but it still seemed a surprisingly abrupt departure with unwelcome undertones of the Canary Island tensions of the past. Janet and I made no attempt to do any work on *Terrapin*. It would have been impossible in the Careenage, so we decamped to a hotel and became totally sybaritic. The honeymoon ended with the realization that we were still 14° south of *Terrapin*'s intended home and the onyx terrapin was not going to take her there single-handed. We sailed at noon on the 11th, setting a course for Cap Moule-a-Chique in St Lucia. "It's only 82 miles" I said. "Simple little run. We'll be there at dawn. Best time to arrive and we'll be all snug by breakfast. Then we'll go back to our bad ways again".

It started well enough and by 2040 we had the loom of the lights of the south coast of St Lucia on the starboard bow, which was reassuring for the south coast of St Lucia is a shipwrecker's dream coast, nothing but millrace seas, headlands, offshore islands, rocks, and sheer cliffs in which the lighthouse at Moule-a-Chique is the one vital linchpin in making a safe landfall. We were set fair. I told Janet to go below and get some rest. Between two and four in the morning I rued the optimism of my departure assurances and was ready to give up sailing, instantly, forever, the minute we landed; if indeed we ever saw land again. A succession of line squalls swept in from the open ocean totally obliterating any indication that land existed anywhere around us, the sea picked up and became unpleasantly sloppy, and somewhere in the middle of all this mess there were two other ships whose lights had appeared briefly and disappeared before I could fix their position and courses. Nightmare? No, just difficult. I had GPS. Then at 0400 the satellites went down. We were no longer fighting a war in Iraq. Continuous GPS coverage was no longer necessary. It was then that the nightmare started. I reckoned first light would come at around 0500 but it was black as pitch, sluicing rain, I was soaking, shivering like a monkey held under a waterfall, I had no idea where we were, and I was getting panicky. I turned due east to pass south of St Lucia, with plenty of sea room I hoped, and woke Janet to take the wheel. I was half dead. By dawn we were standing well out into the Caribbean with the famous Pitons silhouetted against the towering rain clouds five miles away over our starboard quarter. Janet, incredibly, was still smiling. God what a reintroduction to the pleasures of sailing. Would she ever come with me again? We went about, the first time I'd done that since setting out from Cádiz, and headed for Rodney Bay. We were there by 1030. My log ended: "Very tired. 99.8 nm".

Trans-Atlantic landfall? It's got to be Rodney Bay Marina; or English Harbor, Antigua. That's if you're English speaking. If your French is good, you can add in Fort-de-France, Martinique or Pointe-à-Pitre, Guadeloupe. Or, if you're ready to forget the Antilles, the Virgin Islands. That's it. Absolute. There is nowhere else. We spent four nights in Rodney Bay. It's not a pretty place but it's a good marina, and the dull underpinnings of nautical life, engine oil changes, 600 hour services, and scrubbing your underneaths with pot scourers can be undertaken there, simply, quickly, and efficiently. My only vexation was a signal failure to get our shore power hookup working, and for the life of me I couldn't figure out what was wrong with the circuit. Nor could anyone else. What about fun? Yes, oh yes. Let's take it touristically. The Pitons and Soufriere (the accents were lost with the winning of British ascendancy over the French at the end of the 18th Century) are one of the most beautiful island settings in the world: Moorea and Bora Bora win , but the Pitons are something else. If you don't get there by boat, just go to the Humming Bird, have lunch, and take the high road after that, over the neck, towards Vieux Fort. But forget the Sulphur Springs and all that nonsense, it's dreary beyond tolerance, and Louis XVI's mineral baths are about as exciting as a derelict third grade motel. Marigot is great; but spoilt. Where do you go for entertainment? I went to a mega all-night jump-up in the streets of Gros Islet which kept me up until dawn on reggae, rum, and fried chicken. Janet, perhaps wisely, opted out. But at the end of the day there was one curious conclusion we both came to about St Lucia: it has the most stunning scenery but the most scowling faces in the Antilles. I would think twice about buying property there.

It was Saturday when we decided to go French, sail on, and head for Martinique, just over 26 miles away. There is not much to the art of navigation in island hopping by day over that kind of distance. You can see where you're going before you've left, so you just head that way. Then, *whoomf!* you realize that it's not so simple as you move out of the lee of the land and the full force of three thousand miles of Atlantic fetch hits you in the inter-island gap. We were doing over 6 knots and still finding it hard to stay on course. Within 13 miles we had a cross-track error of 2.3 miles left, and I thought "that's it. Lesson learned. In future we'll treat the gaps like the Gulf Stream. Aim way off". We'd sailed at 1145, another of our deliberate late starts, and by sunset we anchored off Anse Mitan, just south of Fort-de-France. I wasn't too happy there, it seemed exposed, so we set two anchors, Cape Verde style, and stayed on board. In any event we hadn't cleared in, so we were still flying our Q flag as well as our French Tricoleur, which hadn't seen the light of day since I sailed from Sète. By the rules you weren't supposed to hit the town before getting your clearances.

The next morning it was all too obvious that Fort-de-France was just too big.

"Do we really want a city?"

"No. Not what we came for. Look at it! It goes on for miles. Even if we try to bike out of it, we'll never make it. They'll kill us. Run us over. The French always drive like hooligans."

"And they won't apologize."

"They never do."

"And they don't even speak English."

On totally unreasonable racist grounds the issue was decided. We'd move on to Dominica.

The north western coast of Martinique is beautiful: a land of tiny villages separated and dwarfed by the corrugations of a vast tropical landscape as the volcanic peaks of the Pitons du Carbet tumble chaotically to the shoreline. High above, the clouds build up, ever changing, and you expect sudden katabatic downdrafts but we had no wind. We were motoring, drinking coffee, and watching as the incredible rounded peaks appeared and disappeared. The 'piton' really is the trademark of these islands, the stuff of travel calendars. If I had an island house, I'd want one with a view of a piton (it's too much to expect to own your private piton) but... then you think of St Pierre and Mount Pelée, and maybe it would be better to forget snugging up too close to the mountain scenery. We could see Mount Pelée in the distance by then, and at midday we were off St Pierre, doing some quick math. How far to Dominica? Say 40 miles to Roseau. At 5 knots? Eight hours. Night landfall? No way. We anchored off St Pierre in 30 ft of water, once again to two anchors, pulled the plague flag down and left the French colors flying. The two anchors were the best decision we made that day.

The horror story of the 1902 eruption of Mount Pelée which destroyed St Pierre, the 'Paris' of Martinique, with the total loss of its population bar a single prisoner locked in solitary confinement, gave its name to the Pelean Phase of a volcanic explosion. The telling of it detracts from the charm of that house with a view of a piton. In an immediate burst of fire, incandescent vaporized rock forms an expanding fireball which soon turns to dense black cloud with a lethal mix of exploding fireballs, searing jets of flame, and lightning. This death cloud, this pyroclastic flow, is heavier than air and hugs the ground as it expands, contouring and moving at speeds of anything up to 200 mph with temperatures as high as 1500°F. At Mount St. Helens the pyroclastic flow flattened forest 17 miles from the volcano and caused all 60 human deaths. All flammable material in the path of the flow is vaporized, carbonized instantly, or bursts into flame. Heat and overpressure causes human bodies to split, if they are not destroyed by carbonization, and the involuntary ingestion of the death cloud (which contains microscopic glass shards) causes severe internal bleeding and later death in any human, animal, or bird still alive. Pliny the Younger wrote of Vesuvius in AD 79 about "a horrible black cloud . . . writhing snakelike and revealing sudden flashes larger than lightning" and then of "the darkness of a sealed room without lights . . . to be heard were only the shrill cries of women, the wailing of children, the shouting of men."

St. Pierre never recovered. You can see the scorch marks on the few standing walls of the old town today, but we didn't go there for ghoulish reasons. My mind was on prehistoric Mediterranean sea power and the Theran eruption in 1628 BC which brought the Minoans to a halt as completely as St. Pierre had been eclipsed and 30,000 people had lost their lives within a single day on May 8th 1902. Today the peaceful appearance of St. Pierre belies the horror and you could wonder that the Minoans were overcome by just one volcanic eruption, but the effect was as devastating as nuclear war. If we needed a reminder of the force of a volcanic eruption we had a doorstep demonstration in Oregon in 1980 when Mount St. Helens blew its top in three places and vaporized 1,227 ft. of mountain cone. There was all the force of a nuclear explosion behind the initial eruption: some said it was 26 times the force of the Hiroshima A-bomb. Others put it higher. Ten miles from the peak a 10 ton caterpillar was blasted 1000 ft by the force of the pressure wave. But Mount St. Helens was a baby. Krakatoa in 1883 was five times more powerful. Thera eclipsed them all.

When Thera exploded a shock wave of superheated air, hotter than molten steel, torched buildings in Crete 70 miles away. The same thing happened at far closer range at Herculaneum when Vesuvius erupted. Wooden beams caught fire instantaneously, only to be extinguished as the city was buried by ash. But long before the Theran ash started falling, slower than the shock wave of superheated air but no less deadly, a wall of water radiated out into the Aegean. We've seen the same effect in our lifetime. On 22 May 1960 an earthquake which caused major damage in Chile also detonated (there's no better word for it) a tidal wave, a *tsunami*, which fanned out into the Pacific. 2,500 miles later the wave hit the south coast of Easter Island at Ahu Tongariki, the site of one of the island's prehistoric temple platforms, where fitted blocks of basalt 475 ft. long and 13 ft. high with fifteen giant 60 ton statues were swept from the foreshore. In the words of Father Sebastian Englert, the island priest who visited the scene later, the statues "were picked up like corncobs and tossed as far as a hundred yards inland." It was worse in the Aegean. Every shore in a direct line with Thera was inundated by a tidal wave which shattered Attica, Argolis, and the Gulf of Salonika, swept 30 miles inland up the Turkish coast, and reached Egypt.

All the Minoan islands, Kea, Crete, Naxos, Kos, Melos, Rhodes, and Cyprus suffered much the same fate: irreparable material damage and the loss of their ships from fire and water, and crippling crop damage from the ash fallout, a knock-on effect which turned the survivors into refugees. Exaggeration? No. Some 38,000 people died from starvation and disease after Krakatoa. In Egypt the ash cloud turned day into night, but that was not until after the Theran *tsunami* had drowned the army pursuing the escaping Israelites as they crossed the Sinai land bridge. In China, one year later, there was a nuclear winter; and the Theran ash cloud must have given the northern hemisphere stunning sunsets for years. Much of the Aegean was left untenanted, open to the thrusting but still primitive Greeks, and the Phoenicians stepped into the vacuum and took over the Minoan sea trade.

The Aegean record of this disaster, the greatest volcanic eruption in three millennia, is still vivid. Sail into the eight mile wide crater of Thera or Santorini, call the island what you will. You are in a caldera a mile deep. Look at the cliffs above you, the rim of the volcano still blazed red by magma from deep in the earth's core which was the initial superheated agent of destruction. Above it, above the red band and the blackened rock, is a white band of volcanic ash up to 160 ft. deep, which is no less than the winding sheet drawn over the Minoan Empire. But for the 1628 BC Thera eruption, the Minoans, rather than the Phoenicians and the Nubian-Egyptians, might well have put their stamp on the Central American civilizations; and the sport of bullfighting, the last lingering shadow of the Minoans, might have reached Mexico three thousand years before the Spanish imported it.

St. Pierre was part of the loop in my civilization thesis, a graphic example of the effect of volcanic power. I think we would have stopped there even if Dominica had been within reach. That night, after midnight, Mount Pelée launched bombshells of wind across the anchorage as if to remind us of its potence. There's a statue of a Virgin on the southern headland which was high above us as *Terrapin* bucked and strained at her anchor rode under the repeated shocks.

"Did you pray to her?" I asked Janet the next morning.

"Yes. You bet I did. Did you?"

"Oh yes. Oh yes."

We were in Roseau Roads by 1400 the next afternoon and it took an hour to moor by the Anchorage Hotel, sore tried by an anchor which wouldn't set until I put on scuba gear and dug it in, with a stern line taken to a tree which appeared to have a root ball about the size of a tulip bulb. We were not alone. Every boat there shared the same precarious kind of arrangement, masterminded by a mafia of local boat boys who had also cornered a lucrative sideline in provisioning. Other than St. Barts, which was a real nightmare, and lying off Port Louis in Guadeloupe one night, Roseau was the least secure place we ever stayed; and yet against all reason, despite 28 knot winds on Night 1, we spent three nights there. Why? Because Dominica was great. Its geography apart, two deprivations have saved Dominica. The first is the lack of an airport which can take medium bodied jets; and the second is the lack of adequate facilities for cruise ships. In time, sadly, this will be rectified and another island will join the chain of Caribbean ports of call that have made themselves so similar that many cruise ship passengers no longer bother to disembark at every stop.

We spent much of our time inland, in the obvious tourist places like the Papillote Rain Forest and Trafalgar Falls. It was Trafalgar Falls that brought me back again to the Mediterranean. If you've read your Plato, you'll know that the central mountain in Atlantis had constantly flowing hot and cold springs, which went a long way to improving their life-style. We know now that on Thera hydrothermal vents were tapped to provide communal hot and cold water systems, including sewage and flush toilets, baths, and showers. If you find it hard to believe all this, go to Trafalgar Falls. The road climbs out of the lush and fertile Padu Valley following the course of a river, and then you really start your climb, on foot, up the jungle-covered crater rim of an old volcano. Clambering over and around massive rocks you scale a near-vertical face down which a 200 ft cascade is plunging just by your left elbow and there, under the ridgeline, two parallel streams of water fall together into a deep pool from a higher precipice: one stream is hot water and the other cold. You can move from cold shower to hot shower as you bathe there, or take your bath, pre-mixed, in the pool. Atlantean luxury! Was Thera Atlantis?

We went into Roseau later that day to find somewhere to dine that evening. The first place we came to advertised its fare on a blackboard hung on the open door:

<u>IN STOCK</u>
Pig Snout
Pig Tail
Beef Navel
Riblets
3 Loaters
Cod Fish
Mackerel
Onions

To our shame we were cowardly and sought out somewhere more sophisticated and so missed our chance to eat loaters, which were obviously a rare catch and, one guessed, highly prized. Later, during our wandering, we telephoned Victoria. To our surprise it was the easiest international call to place we'd yet made.

"Uncle Martin has died." He was the last of the senior generation of my family.

"Do you want us to come back?"

"No. Edward and I will handle it."

But we had to get back. At least one of us should. I should go. I had long been the heir presumptive to our family title, a baronetcy. Clearly now, if family affairs had to be pulled together which I was certain would prove necessary, I had to do it. We couldn't leave *Terrapin* in Roseau Roads. Where could we go? Would Prince Rupert Bay in the north of the island be a safer place? Or should we go on to Guadeloupe? We both got moving. Janet stayed in Roseau to check on flights to London, and I took *Terrapin* single-handed up to Prince Rupert Bay, poised for a quick dash to Guadeloupe or whatever. And there we met twenty four hours later. There was no way anyone could fly from Dominica to London without a lot of chopping and changing, Janet said. We'd be better off starting from Guadeloupe.

We left for the Îles des Saintes the next morning and were there by mid-afternoon, anchored off Bourg des Saintes in a heavy reflected swell which didn't promise well. That night was foul with 25 knot winds. Daylight brought rain squalls every half hour and there were white horses all the way to Guadeloupe. We stayed in the

Saintes. In the morning a 38 ft Warrior arrived that hit a familiar note. It was Paul Booker in *Hannabella* who I'd last seen when we were at the Radio School in Hayling Island together in February 1990, well over a year before. He was going to sail on that day, heading north. We stayed put, not through idleness, just catamaran conscious of head seas. It was another rough night. At 0600 a French 42 footer, *Pelagos*, who had anchored too close to us the evening before, dragged her anchor across our chain and the two anchors became entwined in a festoon of chain and nylon. The anchorage was crowded, chaotic, and it was gusting 23 knots with driving rain. *Pelagos* was crewed by two potbellied sexagenarians and their wives, who patently had no affinity whatsoever with their immediate environment. They made every mistake they could make, and within ten minutes, blind to entreaties, both boats were being blown across the anchorage linked indissolubly by this submarine tangle, both main anchors hanging useless somewhere beneath *Pelagos*, hoisted as high as their electric winch could take the strain. It was an interesting start to the day as at that moment two Club Med four masted cruise ships and *Wind Song*, another of the same breed, arrived in Bourg des Saintes. Three hours later, tucked under the lee of the Îlet a Cabrit, we sorted ourselves out and sailed for Guadeloupe. It was a rough, horrid passage but anything was better than Bourg des Saintes. We reached Pointe-a-Pitre by mid afternoon and collapsed for five days.

It wasn't a total collapse. There was a lot of telephoning at the start and the eventual abandonment of any attempt to fly back to London. Then there was the cruising chute, so mutilated in the run-in to the Cape Verde Islands, to be taken to North Sails and repaired. We'd planned to make for Antigua going outside, around the west coast of Basse-Terre, but then we learned we could cut through the centre of the butterfly that is the shape of Guadeloupe by taking the Riviere Salée up into the Grand Cul-de-Sac Marin and rejoining the Caribbean that way. The only problem was that the one opening road bridge over the river, the Pont de la Gabarre, had been closed since Hurricane Hugo in 1989, but opened briefly at 0500 on Saturday and Monday mornings as a concession to weekend boaters. It was midweek. We thought we might as well wait for the bridge. I think I was slowing down by then: we should have done much more in Guadeloupe with our two extra days, but I never left Pointe-a-Pitre until we set out to anchor overnight by the Pont de la Gabarre, and wait for its dawn opening on the Saturday.

The close vegetation of the banks of the Salée was a little like a throwback to the Petit Rhône, but maybe that was some kind of image transference because I had the crazy delusion that if we spoke to the wildlife we should speak in French. We followed a French keelboat who forced their way past us to be first through the bridge as it opened, closely followed by a large Privilege cat flying an Austrian flag, not an ensign you see every day, with a string of other craft nose to tail behind the Austrians. We debouched into the Grand Cul-de-Sac Marin as if we'd been shot from a circus cannon, far too close to each other, and the French keelboat, cutting corners off the marked channel in their determination to streak ahead, ran aground just south of the Îlet à Fajou. The whole convoy suddenly humped like a python that had swallowed a goat. By then the wind had got up, from the NE, so we had it on the nose, and the fun seemed to be going out of the day. We decided to go to Port Louis, on the west coast of Grande Terre, the eastern wing of the butterfly, and wait for better weather. It was not a pleasant day and not a pleasant night for we were anchored off, there was no guest parking that we could see in the tiny harbor, and the swell coming round the corner from the Atlantic was evil. By 0545 we'd had enough of it and set off for Antigua, thirty seven miles to the north, with two reefs preset ready for the shock of the open ocean. The log says it all:

"Bumpy and unpleasant passage in chaotic seas. Lot of thumping. Violent motion. Lot of water on deck. Glad to arrive."

We anchored in Freeman's Bay in English Harbor at two that afternoon. It was the last day of March. We decided to celebrate the arrival of April by not moving for five days.

Janet loved Antigua. So did I. What did we do? Very little, other than adopt the Copper and Lumber Store Hotel as our local pub and, mindful of Port Louis and other wild anchorages, double the length of chain we had on our main anchor, so that made 50 ft of chain with a 25 lb CQR. I should have done that right at the start. For the rest, it was lotus eating, if that's what you call doing nothing. If we hadn't had a long standing date to meet Vermont neighbors, who were staying with mutual friends in St. Barts, on April 8th, I think we might have remained in English Harbor forever. Part of it, I'm sure, was heavy weather psyche, that leaden reluctance to move on after a bumpy ride. Part of it was simply having a good time. Paul Booker had arrived in *Hannabella*, even the Austrians arrived looking as shattered as we must have done, and we were making new friends each day. To break the spell of our enchantment I proposed that we took *Terrapin* round to Deep Bay on the west coast, so that we were poised ready to take off for St Barts as a straight shot, a run of something like 75 miles right up the Leeward Island alleyway with Antigua and Barbuda on one side, and Montserrat, Nevis, St Kitts, Statia, and Saba on the other. We set out from English Harbor reluctantly, I'll admit that, but we had a fabulous semicircle island cruise and by early afternoon were anchored in Deep Bay drinking Bloody Marys. Morale was sky high. In half a mile of gin-clear turquoise water with a curve of deserted white sand at the end there were just two other boats. The rattling of our yards of chain had seemed overkill as we dropped the hook under the shelter, if shelter were needed, of the northern arm of the bay with its ruined fort. That was April 6th. We'd planned to leave the next day.

"Stay another day? Make a night passage to St Barts and try to get there by midday on the 8th? That'll be soon enough, won't it?"

"You bet."

Our perfect haven didn't remain quite so deserted. The raucous horror of a Jolly Roger pirate cruise shattered the late afternoon for an hour or so, and four other yachts arrived, but Deep Bay is well-named and none of the new arrivals came within a quarter of a mile of us. We discovered too that there was a Ramada Inn on the isthmus at the base of the bay, but it hardly impinged on our adopted territory. For reasons I couldn't divine the Royal Antiguan Resort had been built facing a lagoon, side-on and out of sight of Deep Bay, and, one way or another, the hotel staff must have kept their clientele content with their artificial world. Apart from a mercifully under-patronized ski boat, a woman who spent the day hanging souvenir tee-shirts from the branches of a sea grape and taking them down again, and the scheduled afternoon Jolly Roger visits with their hour of plank walking, we had Deep Bay to ourselves for two days.

The night passage to Saint Barthélemy was idyllic. The lights of Antigua, Nevis, and St Kitts were visible for most of the night as we ghosted along at something like 3.5 knots with just enough wind to keep us moving. The sea was almost oily calm with a slight swell, and the moon came up for the last hours of the night to make it quite perfect. By 0545 we'd sighted St Barts and I've rarely felt more at peace with the world or more relaxed. That was a big mistake. Twenty five minutes later we were hit by 20 knots of wind straight out of the blue, the sea kicked up to moderate then rough, we fought like tiger cats to get the first reef in the main, reefed the genny to the sail numbers, then put the second reef in the main in driving rain, and by then you could only describe it as vicious. St Barts had disappeared. I thought our problems were over when eventually we made the shelter of the island and turned into Gustavia harbor, but I'd forgotten about Mediterranean mooring. It was necessary, I was told when we booked in, to moor stern to, having first dropped an anchor far out in the fairway of the main channel. The positioning of that anchor was vital, it was explained patiently, because there was a strong cross wind and a 'rip tide'. Too true. We were alongside the Harbor Master's quay at that time with *Terrapin*'s flags streaming iron flat in the wind. Prognosis for docking? Not good. Under those conditions a catamaran has the lateral stability of a ball-bearing on ice, and if that weren't enough to contend with, some cruise ship was landing its passengers by tender and a continuous shuttle service of orange lifeboats was ploughing up and down the fairway, churning up wash. If nothing else it set a premium on slick anchor dropping: you had about three minutes between tenders to achieve it and clear the channel. We made it in the end. I can only describe our arrival as a controlled crash which nearly placed my rudders straight through the doors of Hermès. That kind of thing can put you off shopping for a while, and I'm not certain that I ever came to terms with St Barts. Perhaps we had little chance. For three days there was nothing but wind. I wasn't even able to get the main hoisted and flaked down properly, and it remained looking like a bundle of washing, just as it was after our panic reefing that first morning.

"Is it always so windy?" I asked our friends.

"Yes. And it's always rough when you approach St Barts too, on that final stretch." I wish I'd known. We might have taken a rain check on the sea trip and flown in for the weekend. But sadly flying suddenly became the subject of the moment. The son of our Vermont friends was struck by a lightning bolt and knocked from the roof of his Washington apartment to be caught on a lower balcony. He was barely alive, in coma. They flew back to the States that day. Could we help? Yes, they had two younger children, just school age, in Vermont. Janet promised to look after them. St Barts is only served by commuter aircraft so it seemed sensible to take her straight to Sint Maarten to fly out of Princess Juliana airport. What would I do? Take *Terrapin* to the Virgins and leave her there. A day later, after a sharp, rough little passage saved only by a favorable wind, we were anchored in Groot Bai, off Philipsburg, in 8 ft of water with the wind still blowing 18 knots. "Does this wind ever stop in this part of the world?" I wrote in the log as Janet went to fix her airline tickets.

Janet returned ticketed but bursting with more immediate excitement. "Look behind" she said, "look who's out there". The black hull and the red and black funnel with its aerodynamic shielding were unmistakable. It was *QE2*. We'd last seen her in the South Pacific in 1985, when I'd been lecturing on board during a World Cruise. By then her tenders were passing close to us, ferrying passengers ashore. Guessing we knew her Master, Janet sent an invitation by the coxswain of one of her boats. The reply came later over the radio, Channel 16:

"Terrapin, Terrapin, Terrapin.

This is *Queen Elizabeth 2, Queen Elizabeth 2, Queen Elizabeth 2.* Over."

Could he join us? No. They were sailing later that afternoon. With much regret. It was the frantic pace of cruise ship schedules.

I left Janet at the airport at dawn the next morning and felt lost without her. Neither *Terrapin* nor I felt wildly enthusiastic about the next eighty seven miles to Virgin Gorda, for our intended track ran straight across the Sombrero Passage, one of the major connectors, like the Mona Passage and the Windward Passage, between the Atlantic and the Caribbean. All of them have reputations for high seas and high winds. A suggestion came from a Dutch girl working in the chandlery where I was trying to find a handful of oddments. Her boyfriend wanted to go to Tortola to register as a charter captain. He'd sail with me. Barry Hamilton and I sailed that afternoon. By eleven that night we were well on our way with a 23 knot following wind and following seas, both of us still in the cockpit, talking, when I thought I must be hallucinating as a black shape materialized and kept pace with us at head level, just above the port cockpit coaming. Then with a soft apologetic *waaark* an exhausted seabird settled on the horseshoe lifebuoy fastened on the nearest stanchion. Our hitchhiker was there all night, totally unafraid of us and not at all put out by our changes of watches, nor by the bumps as we passed over the Sombrero Bank. At dawn he stirred a little, his feet by then dug well into the coiled line fastened on the top of the horseshoe buoy, but sensibly he didn't spread his wings to warm himself in the heat of the rising sun until the fireball was well over the horizon behind our backs. We'd had the lights of Virgin Gorda in sight from 0215, but the bird thought little of that. It was much later, when the thousand foot peak of the fat virgin was high over our right shoulders as we adjusted course slightly to make

Round Rock Passage, that our bird gave a contented *waaark*, flexed and made some minor adjustments to his wings, and flew away. What kind of bird was he? Neither of us knew, but I'll risk sounding dismissive and uncaring in saying 'no more than a common gull', for I knew he was a Prince in disguise. Someone had only to fall in love with him, and give him a kiss. We both passed on the kissing.

An hour later we surfed through Round Rock Passage, and forty five minutes later we were secured in Virgin Gorda Yacht Harbor at 18° 27'00N 064° 26'12W. It was 0900 hours on April 16th, 1991. Barry went off to catch the next ferry to Road Town. I started putting away the charts I wouldn't need again and the faded photocopy of a magazine article fell out of the pile. I'd forgotten I had saved it. What was its date? July 1988. What was it about? A glowing account of the joys of sailing in the Antilles, titled 'Cruising in Paradise'.

VIRGIN INTERLUDE

Terrapin spent nine months in the British Virgin Islands but she was far from forgotten and certainly not abandoned. In many ways it was fortuitous that Virgin Gorda was the first island you come to as you sail in from the east and I was lucky that Virgin Gorda Yacht Services were there, right at hand, but it wasn't all chance. I'd done my homework in Sint Maarten and decided that it was time to get two of *Terrapin*'s long standing irritants put right while we took time out from our voyaging. I needed to find a small, competent yard in a small island: somewhere I could leave the boat that had become a part of me without worrying about her, content that she was in good hands. A yard where you would know the people you were dealing with and could keep it intimate. And personal. No big islands. No multi-yacht scenes. Virgin Gorda hit the spot.

What was on the agenda? The electrics for a start: that total failure to achieve even a flicker out of an ammeter when hooked up to shore power. While we were tackling that, I thought we might just as well get the whole system sorted out and set up the way it should have been at the start. There's only one way to lay out your main panel and that's to have it set in a door that opens like a cupboard so that you can gain direct and easy access to clearly identified terminal bars. Ideally your wiring should be color-coded. I'd wanted that, but British marine electrical suppliers couldn't achieve it, and a total rewiring was not on the cards in Virgin Gorda. I did get rid of the panel subminiature indicator lights which had failed so often I'd stopped buying spare bulbs, and I went to a Radio Shack for sets of red and green LEDs to replace them. The last requirement on the electrical side was to get the instrumentation right, so that it was possible to monitor AC and DC input from every source, and DC output, full time. Otherwise running a sailboat on a long passage is a bit like running a bank account without reconciling your check book. I can't think why I didn't get that one right in Birdham Pool, but I was running round like a chicken with its head cut off at that time.

What else was on my list? Of coequal importance with the electrics was to remove every trace of the first disastrous sprayhood and bimini arrangement, together with its tangle of canopy bars, framing bars, supporting struts, and tensioning straps; and start all over again. I talked about it at length with Jim Dearing in the Yard. There was only one answer, and that was to go for a hardtop to replace the sprayhood, with forward opening windows. The next step was to make a stainless steel boom gallows, and mount it across the aft cabin coachroof. A bimini could then be secured stretched back from the trailing edge of the GRP hardtop and lashed to the boom gallows, or rolled forward and secured under the lip of the hardtop if you didn't want to use it. After these fundamental decisions had been made, the rest was straightforward and it all came together. The hardtop could be used as a permanent mounting for my solar panels, and could have a cockpit light mounted on its underside. Pluses. The bimini could still be used as a rainwater catchment and take my hose attachment; and

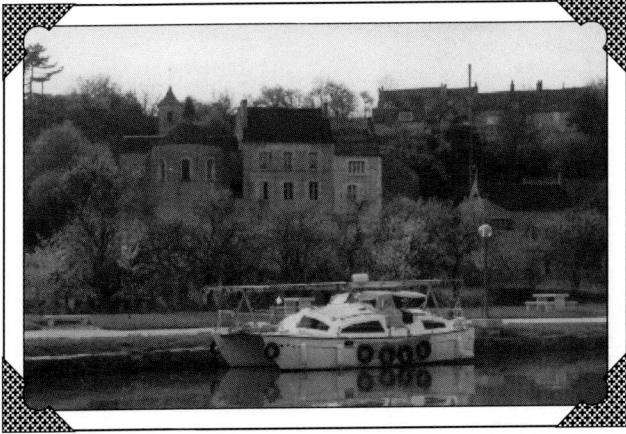

Historic river Seine. Terrapin's mast is unstepped and she wears full French canal protection.

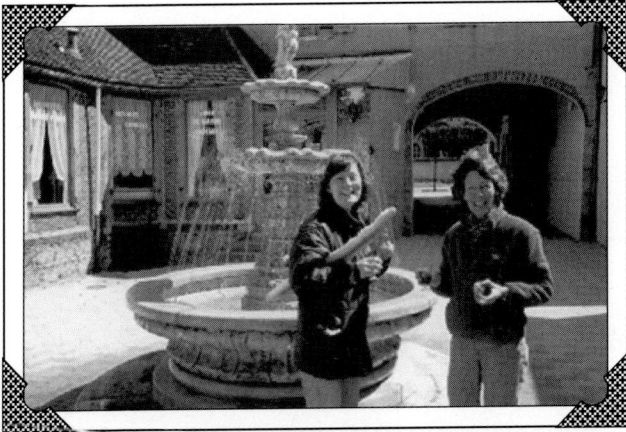

Joigny, on the river Yonne, when the sun came out. George, with the bread, and Janet.

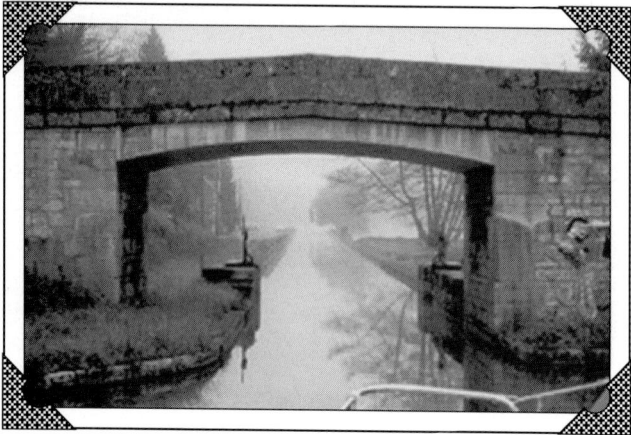

*Some bridges seemed simply too narrow, but
we made it along the Canal du Nivernais.*

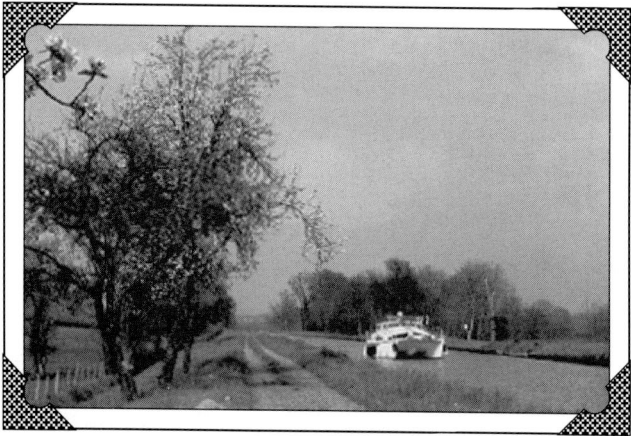

The seagoing Terrapin *seems mammoth and alien
gliding through fields in the heartland of rural France.*

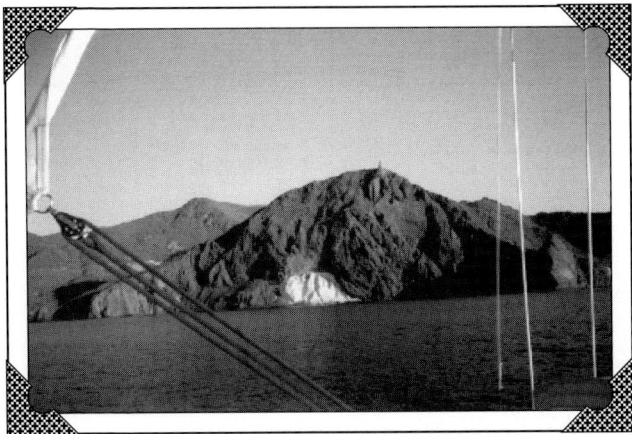

The Costa del Sol: a succession of barren capes.

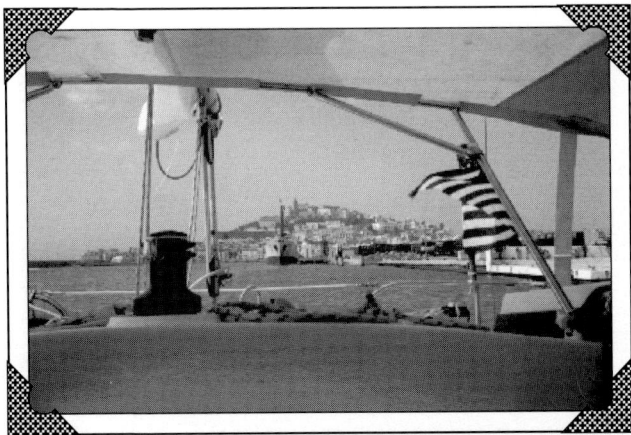

*At Ibiza we put out to sea to find a temporary home
in Spain for* Terrapin.

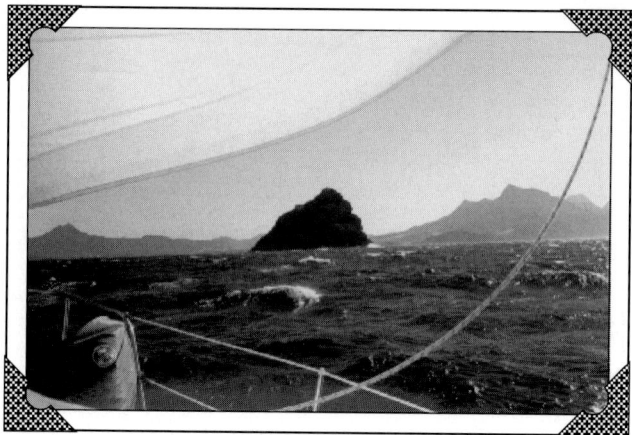

Running into São Vicente, Cape Verde Islands.
The Ilheu dos Passaros is to starboard.

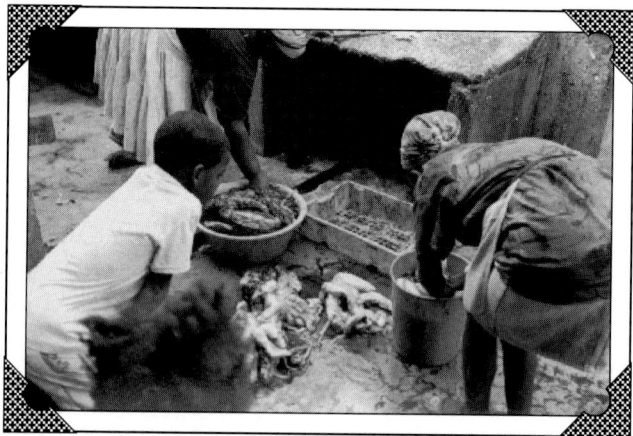

In the Mindelo fish market in São Vicente,
women got the catch of octopuses ready to sell.

Atlantic waves on top of swells. The Ampair water turbine generator is on the starboard stern rail.

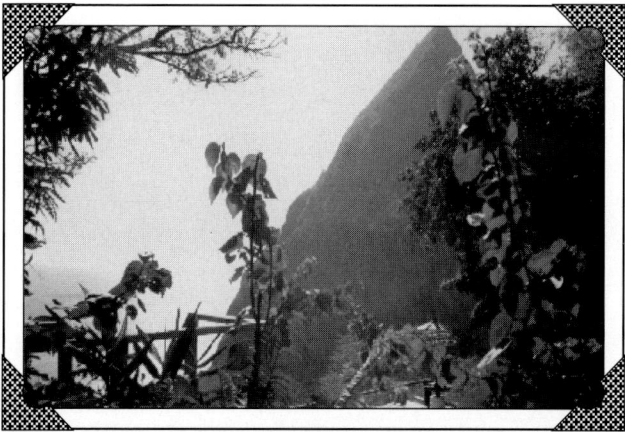

St. Lucia, and one of the famous pitons.

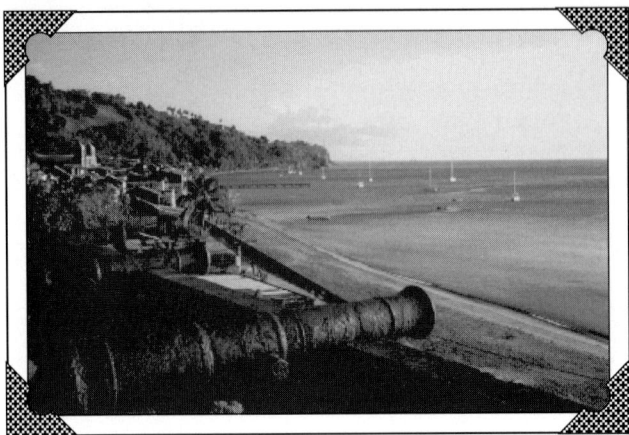

St. Pierre, Martinique. Terrapin *is lying in the far distance, under the headland.*

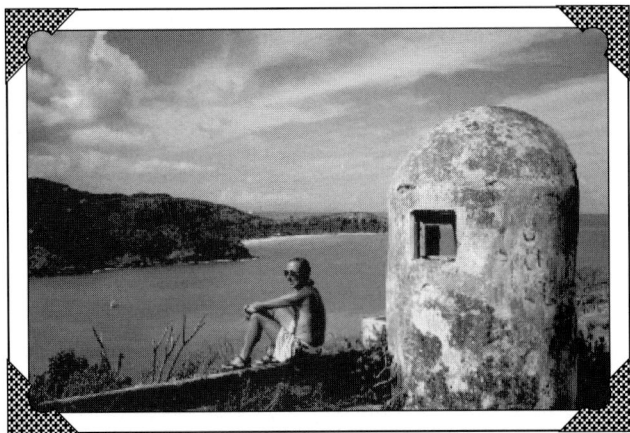

Deep Bay, in Antigua, from the ruined fort. That's the contented skipper, relaxing ashore.

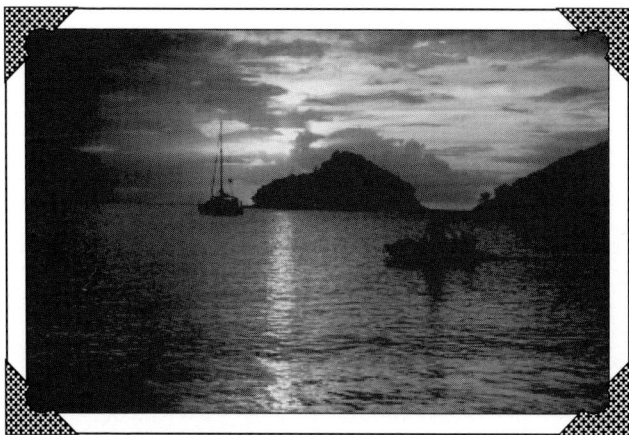

*The darkest shadow in the foreground is me,
returning to* Terrapin *at sunset.*

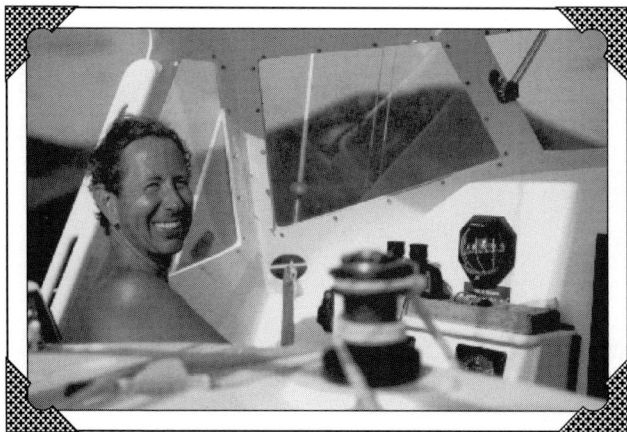

In Terrapin's *cockpit, enjoying the days' sail.
Virgin Gorda Peak is in the background.*

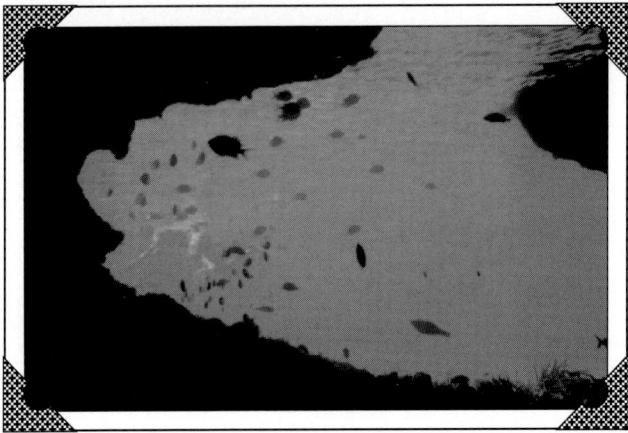

Underwater at Thunderball Cave,
near Sampson Cay, in the Exumas, Bahamas.

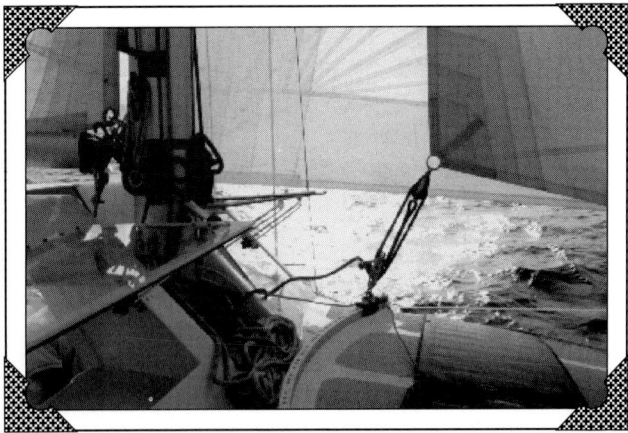

The lines of stitches under strain, with
Terrapin *hard on the wind.*

zip-on side curtains would ensure increased protection and privacy in harbor or at anchor. More pluses. The boom gallows could be fitted with blocks at its base to take the cruising chute sheets (which previously had to share the genoa sheet blocks, necessitating re-rigging each time you used the chute and every time you put it away), as well as vertical cleats to hold the stern lines ready for use on entering harbor, and two eyes to take my trolling lines at sea. The bonuses were accruing.

But before the great refit started, there were plans to be changed. Edith and Victoria Gailey (who had teamed up with us in Paris for two arctic days on the Seine) were due to join us in Virgin Gorda for the next leg, sailing to Puerto Rico and on to the southern Bahamas. Edith cancelled on the point of departure. She was ill. More seriously ill than any of us knew, with cancer. And it proved terminal. But Victoria, her air ticket long set in concrete, flew in to Virgin Gorda, largely unaware of the full import of the changes of the last 48 hours. I could have sailed north with Torey but it would have been, in actuality, single-handing for me and I was wary of the open-water passages up to the Turks and Caicos, and on to the Bahamas. The risks were not justified. Unnecessary. Instead we sailed the Virgins, teamed up with two Canadians who had taken a bareboat charter, James Ludwig and Bernice Rajotte, and I taught Torey to dive. Then we left *Terrapin* and flew to Florida to consolidate her diving with a regular dive course and gain her C-card, for I was only a Divemaster and the PADI's rules forbade my freelancing into the realms of instruction. And then I joined Janet in Vermont. Three weeks later we were in England, deeply involved in family affairs. We didn't return until late June.

I flew back to Virgin Gorda in July. The gallant *Terrapin*, slightly portly and spread at the hips at the start of her life (though I would never have dared whisper it within her hearing), had become a swan. I had nursed a secret dread that we might have got it wrong, we might have triggered off a Frankenstein-like mutation to her lines and produced something that looked like a floating garden shed but the change was more than a significant improvement. I really do believe that the design change at once totally outmoded every boat in her lineage. It remained to try out the sleek remodeled *Terrapin*, for she looked lower, flatter in her silhouette, and far more streamlined without a mass of ill-fitting canvas wrapped around her cockpit.

Edward, our son, flew in with friends and we covered most of the British Virgins in a grand circle tour. After one night of carnival in Road Town and one night of partying in Trellis Bay, we had *Terrapin* so wound up by the excitement of it all and her new good looks that she was sailing faster than she'd ever been before. That day, on our way to dive off the The Dogs, we made 10.7 knots in 22 knots of wind. I found it hard to leave when it was time to pack our bags, and only the realization that it was August saved me from changing my airline ticket. Why August? you might ask. It was the start of the hurricane season, which runs from August through October. Some say it starts in July and ends in December. These are not necessarily no-no months for sailing, but they were not a time I would choose to set out and continue *Terrapin*'s journey north. *Terrapin*, beautiful and much loved though she was, would have to sit it out in Virgin Gorda until November.

By the end of the summer I'd persuaded Janet that her 'last' chance of cruising in the Virgins was too good to miss and that *Terrapin* would prefer to start her journey north in the New Year, rather than immediately. After her sojourn in Virgin Gorda it would be traumatic to move her on too quickly. I thought we'd need a break in any event, for family matters were pulling us back to England in October and early November, and that would be a long haul with a zero fun element. What would we do when we got back to the States? Vermont in November is a definite 'no' and Florida hardly, at that time, a positive 'yes'. There was another cogent reason for waiting until 1992 to take *Terrapin* on the final stage of her journey home. 1992 would be the quincentennial year of Christopher Columbus's discovery of the Bahamas. I could tell Janet was impressed both by the November break idea and the quincentennial voyaging, for she recruited Victoria (our Victoria) to join us in November, and volunteered to join me in Nassau in March 1992 for the final leg to Florida. What I didn't mention, because I thought a pedantic preoccupation with the accuracy of our historical creation was unnecessary, was that Columbus had been in the Bahamas in October 1492, not in March. Much later, by the time Hurricane Andrew had devastated Bahamian island after Bahamian island in August 1992, it confirmed what I'd long suspected: that Columbus was either weather-blind or braver than I thought. Or maybe nobody told him about the no-no months for sailing in those waters.

Would that our November sailing had been perfect. Why was it that every time Janet and I sailed, it turned into an endurance test the like of which you could never imagine? Small wonder that her enthusiasm for sailing was somewhat muted, even in what one might describe as yacht club circles, where a stiff upper lip, or a brave face, whatever it was, was the *sine qua non* of social acceptance. We got nowhere on the weekend of our arrival for the starboard water pump impeller failed and I couldn't get its brass collar off the drive shaft. Perhaps it was just as well for it was blowing 38 knots outside in Sir Francis Drake Channel, so we spent the day holed up in the rocks of Devils Bay and the night at a jump-up in the Bath and Turtle. It might have been the effect of the anesthetic they served at the B&T, but the next few days went swimmingly. It wasn't until we put in to Trellis Bay that the Fates stepped in.

We'd anchored happily enough but during the afternoon the wind got up, blowing straight into the bay, and it was clear that we had to get out of the place. On the way out, you could say at the critical moment as we cleared the nearest rocks, the starboard engine alarm sounded. Impeller again? I had to shut it down. We were motoring, not sailing. There was no way you could sail out against that wind. I couldn't make it on one engine, so I did a quick 180° and tried to find shelter behind Bellamy Cay. When I dived to check that the anchor was well and truly set, I found our chain had fouled an old engine block on the seabed. There was no way that bad weather was going to move us and equally there was no way in which we were going to move anywhere without some serious submarine salvage work. Victoria and I took the Tinker in to the beach to do a surf landing so that I could call Jim Dearing at Virgin Gorda Yacht Harbor and seek his advice about the water pump. Putting out again was interesting for we were passing through the rollers rather than riding over them. Then the outboard failed. That was a new first. By the time I'd got the oars out we were swept onto the rocks. If you are going to get wrecked, it's not a bad idea to do it in an inflatable for there's a measure of bounce in it, but the rocks were not so good for my bare feet and bare legs. One new experience followed another. In the next ten minutes two abortive attempts to get out into deep water failed, we were on the rocks again and then swept against the concrete pier that served Beef Island airport. The pier was worse than the rocks, and there, trying to save us, Victoria gashed her foot and the eight inches of water in the bottom of the Tinker Tramp turned red.

We Tinked over to Bellamy Cay to dine at The Last Resort that night, joining boatloads of tourists all of whom appeared to be living perfectly satisfactory normal lives. Janet had a curious, reserved look on her face which didn't bode well for the great Columbus expedition. Daughter Victoria was surprisingly cheerful for someone who looked as if she'd spent the day being stone-washed in some nightmarish giant drum. There are times when you don't tempt Fate. I thought it better not to announce that the next day would be another new exciting experience. As we left the restaurant Janet within seconds had persuaded two Australians, who by then were feeling no pain, to dive to free our anchor the next morning while I stayed on board ready to keep *Terrapin* off the rocks. To my amazement they turned up. "Worst hangover ever" said one of them. "Can't be worse off down there. Probably better. Cool the head down, won't it Mate?" His mate, suiting up and looking curiously green, never replied.

If you had to pick one cruising ground, where in the world would you go? I've thought about it time and time again. Don't we all? Some of the governing factors are not difficult to lay down: no cold waters for a start. Let's set that limit at once, and keep the ocean temperature at 82°F. While we're thinking of water, let's add in visibility. There will be times when you can't see that old engine block on the seabed because the seas have kicked up, but with my 82°F water I'd add 80 ft visibility as a minimum. Why? Those two 80s march well together, and the combination, over white sand, gives you the colors most people only dream about. What's next? A rush of things. Constant winds, but protected sailing so that you don't get steep seas with the wind. Lots of different islands, so that you've got places to explore, boltholes where, with luck, you can be alone if you want. A safe environment. No piracy. The support of good boatyards, for you always need them. Your own language. Even your own currency. A place that offers easy access by air, and is relatively close, nowhere Light Years away on the other side of the world. It's not surprising that the Virgin Islands are one of the most popular cruising grounds in the world. They top my list.

Yes, there are too many people cruising there. Cooper Island is not much fun when there are 37 yachts anchored off Machioneel Bay, and The Bight at Norman Island with 57 yachts getting backwinded and fighting for space is about as attractive as the New Jersey Turnpike on a winter Friday night. But you learn to work around these things. You've got to, for the only real alternative is to take off to Polynesia and cruise in the Society Islands; and, if you do that, you'll be disappointed. There are wall-to-wall people there too. To answer my own question, I think the Number One cruising ground has got to be the Virgin Islands. With two caveats. (1). Don't be around there when the whole of Puerto Rico decamps in the early summer in their sports fishermen to party in the Virgins for a week: run if you hear that annual fiesta coming your way. And (2). Avoid the Christmas Winds.

You wouldn't even want to send someone you disliked sailing when the Christmas Winds were blowing. Would you?

AVOID LONELY ISLANDS

Virgin Gorda, British Virgin Islands, to Nassau,
Bahamas. January 29 - February 29 1992

For weeks I'd been suffering from tactical astigma-
tism, staring at the chart like a rabbit watching a cobra,
quite unable to decide how to get from Virgin Gorda to
Jupiter Inlet. I can't think why I found it so difficult, but
I found myself weighing the merits and demerits of every
inter-island passage. It was about as productive as the
theological debate about the number of angels who could
dance on the head of a pin which had once brought
Constantinople to a standstill. In the end I plonked my
parallel rules down on the big chart, one end on Virgin
Gorda and the other on Jupiter lighthouse, and went that
way. The names read off in a straight line, albeit with
some minor jinks: Puerto Rico, the Turks and Caicos
Islands, the Plana Cays, and the Exumas to Nassau.
Would Janet join me there? After that she could choose
the route.

I can't recall when it was that I first persuaded
Alice, my cousin and goddaughter, to take on the first leg
to Puerto Rico. I think she'd been talking of sailing off
her native Suffolk coast, which I'd always remembered
as a questionable pursuit if you were looking for plea-
sure, nothing but layers of grey greased wool sweaters
and yellow oilskins, so it must have been in London, way
back, that I'd started painting the colors of the tropics.
She was working in an art gallery, so the brushwork
seemed appropriate. Thank Heaven Virgin Gorda in

January lived up to the dream. No Christmas Winds. It was almost the other way round. No wind at all. By the time we reached Road Town to clear out of the British Islands, *Terrapin*, thoroughly put out by motor-sailing, sheared her port engine stop cable. I spent most of the next day replacing the cable while Alice gave herself a Do-It-Yourself course on handling an inflatable, which had Village Cay Marina electrified in its early stages and certainly promoted a brisk mid-morning bar trade in Pain Killers, the near-lethal Virgin Island rum cocktail.

We were ready to set off again. On the spur of the moment we decided to check Norman Island for space on our way to Charlotte Amalie and found The Bight surprisingly empty, so we stayed to dive the Treasure Point caves. We surfaced to find a familiar charter yacht arriving, *Windward Dream*, who Janet and I had last seen in English Harbor. By then the sunset promised to be brilliant, flaming Pinatubo reds and purples (the sky painting effect of the 1991 eruption of Mount Pinatubo, caused by particles of dust carried high into the atmosphere), so we stayed on to meet Neil from *Windward Dream* on the Baltic Trader restaurant boat, the *William Thornton*, which is anchored in The Bight; and Eddy, who I'd known from my previous visits, was there running the ship-restaurant. We played tapes and drank Heineken and talked, and no-one even attempted to solve any problems. All of this is trivial, not the stern stuff of passage-making, so why do I mention it? Simply because days like this are the casual, easy way good cruising goes, not just an antidote for traffic fumes and inner city decay, but the antithesis of the whole ethos of 'normal' life in our western developed nations. Escapism?

The next day was mirror calm, the sea metallic, and you felt you could have walked to St Thomas. We motored slowly past St John and for the first time, in perfect conditions, I calibrated my log against the GPS. I felt enormously proud of myself and professional when I'd done it. After that heat exhaustion set in. It was like sitting at the bottom of a wok covered with a glass lid out there, even under the bimini, and the reflected glare from every side could have given an elephant a sun tan. By the time we docked at the Ramada Yacht Haven Marina, much impressed by the long lineup of cruise ships we passed on our way in, we felt as if we were totally dehydrated. We just made it to the Bridge Bar before a state of total collapse set in.

Charlotte Amalie, I'd told Alice, was a serious port-of-call. Not lotus-eating. I'd decided that the two folding bicycles I'd bought for the French canals were not earning their keep, and wherever I stowed them I lived to regret it. There was just too much bicycle on one small boat. In France, on the canals, we'd used them every day and the foredeck was fine as a parking area. Later, in the Mediterranean and during the Atlantic crossing, they were in the cockpit which made it a little crowded with the eight 2-gallon water cans and the cruising chute, but I had no dive tanks on board at that time, so we got by. If nothing else you could reassure yourself that it cut down the space in the cockpit. Better if you were going to get pooped. Less weight of water. But in the islands it became another story, and to my surprise I found that we never used the bikes. It was not that we were idle. We walked for preference; and in Virgin Gorda we rented a jeep for a day if we wanted to go further afield. I wouldn't have enjoyed pushing my bike up Virgin Gorda Peak, nor, I think, the screaming excitement of the precipitous ride down the far side.

"We're in the States now" I told Alice. "We can go to a Post Office and mail them to me in Florida. We'll clear Immigration first, and get it done by nine in the morning. Then we can explore".

If you're in the business of clearing in ships like Carnival's *Ecstasy* with 2,700 passengers and 900 crew, a cockleshell with two on board, even if it does have a tiny onyx terrapin in a Vermont cherry case, doesn't rate high in your priority list. That was Day 1. But by Day 2 we'd figured out the bike mailing business. The first stop was the nearest supermarket to collect empty cardboard boxes so that we could cut them up to make our own packaging, and to buy yards of tape. If you are taking on casual crew during your passage-making, I suggest you check them out for bicycling ability first. I saw no reason why Alice should run me down at a busy intersection at the foot of a steep ramp as we left the supermarket, and her claim that she couldn't see past the four boxes balanced on her handlebars was no more than an admission of poor organization. It took an hour to get to the Post Office, which seemed excessive for it was barely a quarter of a mile, but Alice did have a puncture on the way and I ran into a roadside tree when I looked back to see why she was no longer with me. The packaging only took an hour and a half. We had to borrow scissors from the Post Office, that had been a foolish omission, but then I'd been concentrating on the concept of the plan rather than minor detail. We squatted like Indian *babus* on the verandah, cutting and taping cardboard with a circle of admirers around us much of the time as the sun rose higher and higher in the sky, and it seemed that the US Virgins were locked into another day of heat wave. At the end, despite the fact that the bicycles were perfect twins, we'd produced two totally dissimilar, damp, misshapen cardboard humps. The miracle was that the Post Office accepted them, but perhaps they were only too pleased to get their scissors back. I'm a great fan of the US Postal Service. The bicycles reached Jupiter weeks before *Terrapin*, and for the first time we could sit at the saloon table.

The next day we left for Culebra and the wind was back, right on the nose. We had no option but to motor, and when we got there, seeking shelter, felt our way hesitantly into the Canal del Sur to anchor under the lee of the Cabeza de Perro. I had thought originally of going into the Ensenada Honda, which on the face of it seemed the obvious target, but something I'd read somewhere had put me off, so I felt disinclined to start proving the validity of advice just as the sun was setting behind the mountains of the central spine of Puerto Rico, which by then was dominating the western horizon. Our refuge was fine, apart from a single oversized attendant barracuda who wouldn't leave *Terrapin* alone and two Puerto Rican sports-fishing boats whose crews might have won prizes in the very large family stakes. The Puerto Ricans were so totally absorbed in practicing their partying techniques for the great annual run to Virgin Gorda that they never even noticed our anchoring. We were left on our own in the isolation of a party of three: two newly confirmed non-swimmers and our faithful barracuda.

I'd heard that Vieques Sound was a cruising lake, a dream area for small boats, and the kind of place you wanted to play around in for a few days. If your next leg was out into the Atlantic, crossing the Puerto Rico Trench, the Mona Canyon, and passing by the Navidad and Silver Banks on your way to the Turks and Caicos, it seemed to me that a day or two of play time was in order. The waypoints ahead were names of some significance. I thought of my Russian "nobody knows what will be tomorrow" and outlined an idea.

"It's midweek, so we should have the place pretty much to ourselves. No practice party runs going on. Let's leave Culebra and go to Palominos (a set of palm-fringed dream islands off the Fajardo coast) and then tomorrow we might head south to look at Vieques itself. But the island has a danger zone. It's used as a naval firing range or something. We'd better watch that. We don't want to be taken as a target sampan. It could spoil our day."

Alice went forward to take in the anchor and I heard her explaining the plan to the barracuda. I just hoped that he wasn't a long distance swimmer or a born traveler. The sky was darker than it ought to have been but I thought it was no more than the souvenir of a pre-dawn line squall. We had no sea running and almost no wind, and it was looking as if we would be motor-sailing all the way. Maybe I was too close to Culebra? Maybe I ought to pull south, so that we were open to the Trades which should have been coming in right behind us, whoomping along past the Virgin chain. We were starting to rock a bit as I was figuring it out, in a swell that was coming straight round the corner of Culebra, hitting us on the starboard bow; and then the wind came. It was nothing at first, 16 knots, a moderate breeze, but as we cleared the shelter of Culebra it built up. Force 5. Force 6. From the north west. The wind we could handle, we'd got plenty of sea room in Vieques Sound, at least for the moment. The reefs closed in as you approached the Puerto Rico coast, but that was way ahead. At that time I had just two problems. The first was the beam seas which were building up, worse than I could have believed for they shouldn't have been there, at least not quite that way. When you next fly from San Juan to the Virgin Islands, look down as you cross the coast of Puerto Rico. There's a chain of islands and reefs running from Cabo San Juan, its north eastern point, all the way to Culebra. Geologically it's probably part of the Virgins, but whatever it is, the barrier chain known as La Cordillera shields Vieques Sound from the open ocean. You can see, looking down from your aircraft seat, that you'll get Atlantic wind in the Sound but not the swells, not the waves. They break on La Cordillera. And were they breaking that day: great sheets of spray as the successive walls of ocean water hit the rocks but it didn't end there, for they seemed to reform and carry on. Either my topography was at fault or you can take a rain check on Vieques Sound as a play area if it's a Cordillera-busting day. Something really foul must be happening or have happened way out in the Atlantic. Something Force 10 or even more.

What was the other problem? I felt ill. Really ill. We'd been motor-sailing and it was the old problem of *Terrapin*'s exhausts, which should have been taken further aft and angled. If the wind came just so, the diesel fumes came into the cockpit. My ancient susceptibility to seasickness had been largely eroded by some ten months of sea time on board *Terrapin*, but diesel fumes were a real killer. I pointed out the main island of Palominos, looking with its tuft of palm tops like a black shoe brush on the horizon, and told Alice to kick me when she could start counting tree trunks with my binoculars. I did a 360° survey. We were OK otherwise. There was a well-formed waterspout to the south but that was downwind. I added she'd better keep an eye on that too. Then I stretched out on the cockpit floor and went comatose. By then we were well into Day 1 of our designated Play Time in Vieques Sound, Puerto Rico.

Palominos was a no-no. It was dangerous there when we arrived and the weather was still deteriorating. Alice was due to fly out from San Juan and the Canadians Torey Gailey and I had teamed up with during our Virgin Island cruising in April were flying in to join me, ready to sail on to George Town in the Exumas. At the back of my mind I'd thought I might take *Terrapin* into San Juan harbor for it would be handy for the crew changes, but that idea was out of the window. The story of a inshore passage off northern Puerto Rico in the conditions we had that day wasn't the sort of tale you'd want to add to your Ancient Mariner repertoire, for you wouldn't be around to tell it. Where else could we go? The closest port. Fajardo. Two hours later I was having doubts about that too. We put into Puerto Chico, the first marina we came to, and the surge was wicked as we secured to the fuel dock. The place was deserted. No-one around. Just a lot of wildly rocking boats. At last I roused the pump attendant. In Vermont, kindly, he might have been described as being 'two bricks shy of a full load'. Nothing was right there and we left to try Villa Marina, the only alternative. Its entrance lay up a narrow dredged channel which in the surge was a bit like one of the waterchutes at Florida's Wet and Wild amusement park. In the end we tucked ourselves well up into the marina, safely netted in cat's cradle of lines, and went off to check the facilities. I don't know whether a cold drink, a real one, with ice in it, or a hot shower was No 1 on my list of priorities right then. No ice. And the shower? You could use one of two words: 'primitive' or 'basic'. And then add a third word. 'Cold'.

If I'd been in the guilt and remorse business, I would have had Alice's cruise in paradise branded on my conscience as surely as Mary Queen of Scots was said to have 'Calais' branded on her heart when she died. There are some sailing partnerships that work and it was a pity to see it end, two days early, in the Villa Marina, Fajardo. Vieques Sound had been something. I wasn't going to pretend for one moment that it could be offset against being knocked off my bicycle under the wheels of a taxi in Charlotte Amalie, but something had to be said after our cold showers.

"What about offshore next year? You'd better find a course somewhere first, nothing much, but just brush up on some of the 'this is the sharp end, this is the blunt end' stuff."

"OK."

"It's selfish on my part, I know, but Vieques Sound was spoiling. I rather like sleeping on passage. Just get it so that I can take the odd nap every now and again?"

"Where are we going? Easter Island?"

Unlikely, but who can tell? What I could offer was a more immediate reward.

"What would you like to do here?"

The answer was to see a Rain Forest. So I rented a car and we went to tour El Yunque. At the end of the visit neither of us had any doubt why it was called a rain forest and Alice flew out of San Juan, I hope, content.

Jim Ludwig lived in Calgary and was having his dream boat, *Shalena*, built in British Columbia. He and Bernie Rajotte, before taking off in one of the great marine leaps we all so foolishly decide we're going to take, were building up sea time. The Tinker Tramp hadn't been rigged as a survival craft for years it seemed, and I'd almost forgotten how to set about it. Instructions in hand we achieved it, and in a repeat of Puerto Sherry, did a trial squeeze. It was a squeeze. Jim's a big man, and when I say that, I mean a BIG man, and Bernie, though diminutive beside him, had bumps and curves in all the right places. I don't think we would have suffered from hypothermia under that canopy and our combined weight had the air out of it, and the Tink re-rolled, within minutes. We were ready to go.

Deep down secretly I was a little scared of the next leg. It was that lee shore, the northern coast of Puerto Rico, for a start, the reputation of the immediate sea area, and the repeated, insistent advice I'd had from everyone I'd consulted to keep well out from the Navidad, Silver, and Mouchoir Banks. Looking at the chart, our projected track appeared to be nothing less than running the gauntlet past a lot of places which, on a mediaeval chart, would have been marked with sea monsters and maelstroms. Right at the start our leeway took us too far to the west and I had to offset by another 15°, but then we settled down on a satisfactory course. The seas were sloppy, confused after the big storm, and infrequent rain squalls blotted out what was left in sight of the mountains of Puerto Rico. We achieved 120 nm in that first 24 hours which wasn't too bad, and were then slowed down as the wind dropped. By late afternoon the second day we were in a shipping lane with three ships within visual range when the wind died. We started to motor, which was no bad idea for the batteries were low. Neither the wind generator nor the solar panels were having any effect on our battery state and I suspected a major corrosion problem in my through-deck fittings. You could say that it was a so-so start, pretty much par for the course, in putting out to sea again. There are always some glitches. As if in compensation we did catch a 4 1/2 ft dorado that day; and then perversely I suffered from the most terrible sadness after watching the quick-flashing iridescent aurora of its death agony and I put my deep sea line back in the fishing locker. By Day 3 we were off the Navidad Bank, and the next day, with something like 24 hours to run to Grand Turk Island, we were off the Silver Bank. I was asked later, long after my return, why I hadn't gone closer to the banks to see the whales, for the three areas of shallows form the winter habitat of the New England whales. I could only say it was my cowardly frame of mind. Somehow we weren't in a whale-watching mode right then, and my one concern was to make a safe landfall at Grand Turk, keep off the reefs, and get safely past South Caicos into the more protected waters of the Caicos Bank. If you're inclined to skimp in your chart buying, you don't try to economize over your Turks and Caicos charts. You buy large scale charts, every chart you might conceivably need, and you keep your fixes going as if your life depends on it. I think it does. Let me just quote from one pilot: "From about northeast around to southwest the coast of Grand Turk is fouled by off-lying reefs extending from a mile to 10 miles off . . .". That kind of report can stimulate your interest in navigation.

I wanted to be off Grand Turk Island at dawn so that I had a full day to turn down the Turks Island Passage and get round South Caicos. Thereafter I reckoned we'd have to anchor off, in the middle of the Caicos Bank, for one night. Sailing on would be too dangerous because of the coral heads. Provided it didn't blow up, we'd be fine. We'd make Providenciales, our target, the next day. By 0500 we were four miles due north of Grand Turk Island in deep water, right on the 1,000 meter contour, and we held that line as we turned south west and were swept into the millrace of the Turks Island Passage, which runs between Grand Turk and the Caicos Islands. I've been told that it's a Whale Interstate Highway during their annual migrations, but we saw no whales that day. By 0900 wind, wave, and current had us at the witching point, the place where you've got to decide how you're going to get through the reefs and get on to the Caicos Bank. The timings were good. We needed the sun high in the sky but still behind us for eyeball navigation, for there comes a time when you must set the charts aside and get someone to climb the mast wearing Polaroids. None of my sailing directions seemed to make it very clear which was the best way to go, or maybe I was stupid and couldn't get the hang of what they were saying, but it took us longer than I wanted to work it all out. I can only say that the next two and a half hours were interesting, and then, at last, we were on the Caicos Bank.

I don't know whether the Caicos Bank is the largest lagoon in the world, but I'd certainly describe it as the world's largest swimming pool. What have you got there? An area of water, 60 miles across and averaging around 12 ft deep, ringed in part by a string of fringing reefs and cays, with the larger islands of the Caicos group to the north. Outside this incredible circle the sea bed plunges to ocean depths within yards. Seen from a satellite it must look like a turquoise set in a field of midnight blue, for the waters over the Bank have the brilliant clarity of a stone under a jeweller's spotlight. One shouldn't get too excited, for it's not a flawless jewel. The brown striations and flecks you see are coral ledges and isolated coral heads, which are likely to do more than take the barnacles off your bottom unless you avoid them. We set out across the Bank at 1130 and by

1730 we decided it was time to stop. By then we were completely out of sight of land. It's an extraordinary feeling to drop anchor in 12 ft of water with no land in sight in any direction, even from the masthead; but it would be suicidal to continue on your way through the night. By 1230 the next day we'd secured in the Caicos Marina and Ship Yard, a treeless wasteland of new pilings, temporary huts, and blinding white sand. Yes, they were still building the place. Where were we? Miles from anywhere, it turned out. Did it matter to be so far out of Provo? The answer is that it was more than inconvenient to be so isolated, but we needed a yard. Not only were there the through-deck connections from the solar panels and the wind generator to clean, but the toilet had jammed on the second day of the passage. We'd got by without it. You have to, don't you? It's back to a bucket half-filled with salt water, or you hang from the swimming ladder, which more often than not will give you a douche at the same time. It's not as hazardous as it sounds. Remember the clip-on rules?

It took all of one day to succeed and fail. The electrics were fine by the end of the morning. It was corrosion. There was no visible evidence of it whatsoever until you stripped down each through-deck fitting. Another lesson learned. The toilet was the failure. I was hot, angry, and totally frustrated by the end of the day. I called Janet, gave her a list of spare parts, and asked her to ensure that John Higginson, our long time Vermont neighbor who was joining me in George Town, brought them with him. Thank Heaven Jim and Bernie had got a rental car and we went out to eat. I needed a break. We should have left the next morning so that we had time in hand to reach George Town without the stress of an approaching deadline, and so that we had the sun behind us, or above us, as we made our way westwards to leave the Caicos Bank by way of Sand Bore Channel; but Jim and Bernie wouldn't hear of it. I'd been working all the day before. Now they'd got a car and they were going to take me around Provo. We'd have lunch. Then leave. I don't think I was an idiot to agree, but I was a fool not to delay our departure by 24 hours. If only I could say that Provo appealed to me after our circle island tour, but there's little to see but scrub and rock, all of it low lying and sun-baked, scarred by new roads and new developments. You would have to be a beach freak or a diving fanatic to even think of buying property there.

We had to gain a two mile offing out over the Bank before we could turn west, and right at the start it was a slow crawl over the ground as we ran straight into 15 knot winds and steep little head seas. By the time we reached our turn point you didn't have to look at your watch or the chart to know that making the Sand Bore passage in daylight was going to be a close-run thing. Why didn't I turn back? I can't think. I must have lost my marbles that day. Sand Bore Channel is a half-mile wide break in the reef between Provo and West Caicos Island. It's unmarked, unless you call the wreck of a ship on the reef on the north side a kind of mark, and the only way to find it is by clearing the South Bluff of Provo by about two miles, holding 278° for a while, and then going by the color of the water. The fireball of the setting sun was low over the horizon, right in my eyes, when we reached the critical point and the colors in the water were obliterated. It didn't help that GPS was down. "Classic example of how not to set about it" I wrote later in the log "time too tight, light wrong, everything wrong". We reached ocean waters just as the fireball disappeared. It was one of the few sunsets in all my voyaging that no-one bothered to look for the Green Flash.

I guess the stress of our departure was the cause of the next potentially lethal snafu. Jim and I had a good system of navigation going in which we each worked out our course and timings from an agreed list of waypoints, and we each worked out the position of our waypoints. Then we double checked our independent workings, programmed the GPS, and marked the chart with our intended track. We were doing this as soon as we were clear of Sand Bore Channel and somehow we got the position of the first waypoint wrong by 1°. It should have been 22°17'N and we were working off 21°17'N. No big deal, you might say, thinking of your school geometry: but a degree of latitude is 60 miles. Neither of us picked it up. Our intended course was north west, to pass to the west of Mayaguana on our way towards the Plana Cays, and stupidly I never realized that we must have had the wrong heading when I set our initial course. At midnight I handed over, confident that we were on course. We were on the course as set: but the programming of that first leg was critically wrong. When I came back on watch at 0800 the next morning I found, to my horror, that not only had we been sailing south west, but we'd passed between Little Inagua and Great Inagua islands during the night. There were only two conclusions to be drawn.

The first was that the fault was mine entirely. The second was that it was not in the cards that the three of us were due to die on an Inaguan reef that night.

There was a knock-on effect too. We'd lost eight hours, we were 18 miles south and 46 miles west of our Sand Bore Channel exit start point, and we had 206.79 nm to run to reach George Town. The only ameliorating factor was that our longitude was acceptable. All we had to do to pick up our planned track was sail almost due north on 349° Magnetic for 65 miles, but it meant there would be no play time on the rest of the passage, and my plan to visit Samana Cay, which I've always thought must have been Columbus's first landfall (not San Salvador, nor any of the other seven contenders for the distinction) was probably unachievable. Jim and Bernie had flights booked out of Great Exuma on Friday morning, which gave us four days up to their check-in time, on the face of it, more than enough time to cover the distance to George Town. But once we got to the north of Long Island, around Rum Cay, night sailing would be out of the question. There were too many reefs around after that point. The blue water phase would be over. And the weather?

The weather was not good on the first day which I awarded a 3 on my 1-10 scale and a zero for fun, but we reached the Plana Cays by 2130 that night. Then, having served our penance, everything was beautiful. We had a magic sail through the Plana Passage under a full moon, and the next day, as we ran north paralleling the coast of Long Island, was perfect. We sunbathed, hung up the sun shower, shampooed, started fishing again, and did some more sunbathing. Our only task, if you can call it that, was deciding where to drop the hook that night. We pored over the charts and guides. It had to be somewhere round the north end of Long Island, for there was nowhere on the north east coast. That meant rounding Cape Santa Maria well out to sea, for the reefs extended something like three miles out from the cape. So far so good, but you didn't have to be a boy genius to know that we'd be rounding Cape Santa Maria at about 2030 and, having turned the corner, getting in to anchor around the 3 Fathom Line meant getting inside the outlying reefs. There were two options: to sail on into Exuma Sound and heave-to somewhere, or to find a feasible approach to a safe anchorage. I chose Calabash Bay. The gap in the reef was well documented and the met was right: the wind was perfect, visibility was perfect, and it would be a full moon night. What was necessary was to construct a perfect approach matrix from a waypoint to the north east of Cape Santa Maria, and then follow it exactly, leg by leg, until we were inside the bay in anchor depth. It was, in many ways, a therapeutic exercise after the Sand Bore Channel fiasco, but I don't go navigating through reefs at night just to recover my self-esteem. And I wouldn't have attempted it without GPS. I checked the satellite schedule and we would have continuous coverage during the critical period.

Jim lay flat on the foredeck with a powerful flashlight, which, if he had to use it, would be used so that the beam of the light was outside my field of view and wouldn't spoil my night vision. Not that night vision was going to be acute that night with a full moon, but you take no chances. The CQR was ready, in the bow roller, with the chain flaked out. Bernie was beside me, reading off the distance we had run, the depth, and, on the final leg, the seconds of longitude. I concentrated on my heading and on a highly tuned in-built personal panic sensor. Before we went to action stations during the first leg, off Cape Santa Maria, we'd taken in the sails and started motoring. Slowly, slowly we went in on the final leg on a course of 090°, exactly due east. We were in the lee of the island, there was no wind, and it was almost millpond calm. The only sound was the low resonance of *Terrapin*'s engines. At exactly 2315 we dropped the anchor in 15 ft of water at 23°39'16N 075°20'52W. We slept late and left for George Town at 0945. We were there five hours later with a day in hand.

Our safe anchorage after rounding Cape Santa Maria stayed much in my mind, albeit subliminally. There are many Columbus-associated names in the Bahamas, some false, some true, but the name Santa Maria should have rung a bell and I should have checked his log when I got back to the States. It slipped my mind until a year later when I was reading Paul Chapman's reanalysis of the First Voyage, *Discovering Columbus*. Suddenly the somewhat terse account came to life and I was back there, creeping into Calabash Bay just as Christopher Columbus, on passage from Great Exuma Island to Long Island on Wednesday October 17th 1492, had felt his way into the same anchorage:

> I sailed to the north-north-west . . . Two
> miles from the cape there was a wonder-
> ful harbor . . . I anchored outside and we

> went in with the ship's boats . . . It had
> no depth . . ."

His caution was well founded. Martin Pinzon, the captain of the *Pinta*, had been warned by the natives of the Exumas that Long Island should be rounded well off to the north-north-west, and the draft of the Columbian vessels, though not great at something around seven feet, was still too much for relaxed sailing in Bahamian waters. It must have set a premium on eyeball navigation, set a high value on the utility of a ship's boat, and certainly dictated day sailing unless they were well offshore. Getting into Calabash Bay in *Terrapin*, with her twin diesels, sailing instruments, and GPS was child's play. Whatever your opinion of Columbus, he was a seaman.

George Town is heaven and hell. It is the end of the line for those who cruise in the Bahamas and the springboard for those who are heading south to the Caribbean. Inevitably, like any decision point, it has attracted a semi-permanent population of those who have either run out of steam or run out of courage. It serves its population, both the transients and the yacht squatters, well. The supermarkets are good, the drinking atmosphere is convivial, and the food is fine. There are just too many boats, and, by extension, too many people. I found myself becoming increasingly irritated by the proprietary attitude of the 'permanent residents' and their interminable VHF radio morning chat sessions typified everything I went to sea to escape. I lasted four days in George Town. I had to, for John 'Higgy' had to arrive and I had to repair the toilet, fix an aft cabin fan, and the solar regulator which had been in a state of febrile instability since Calabash Bay. And we needed diesel and water.

Terrapin had covered 791 miles since leaving Virgin Gorda and we were roughly 350 miles from Jupiter Inlet. Nassau was only 135 miles away, and John had booked to fly out of there on March 1st. Janet was flying in two days later, and we'd do the last 200 mile leg together. In the meantime our seven day trip up the Exuma chain was to be nothing but a dalliance with lots of swimming, and lots of diving. We set out on Sunday February 23rd, sailing up the Exuma Sound under the cruising chute and switched across to the Bahama Bank through Rudder Cut. We spent the first night anchored in a low tide depth of 3 ft of water between the Darby Islands. We'd covered all of 31 miles. I wouldn't claim that we were overstressed by our first day. You could say the second day was as taxing. We made it all the way to Staniel Cay, running about 2.5 miles off the cays, and clocked up all of 25.9 nautical miles. We went on to find Thunderball Cave the next morning, the place where part of the movie *Thunderball* was shot. With both of its entry points underwater, it took some time after we'd anchored before we'd located the main entrance. Going in was stunning. It was sensational, better than we'd dared hope, with its fish population, unafraid and incurious, hanging suspended in brilliant midnight blue water shot with a topaz shaft of sunlight which comes slanting down through the hole in the dome of the cave. After diving Thunderball twice and running out of film, we made it on to Sampson Cay. The day's run? Just 4.14 miles. John, who flies, was much taken with the two Maule seaplanes we found there in the inner harbor and I reckoned the whole place was pretty close to the heart's desire. We seemed to be the only visitors, which was odd for Staniel Cay had been bursting at the seams, but we took it as good fortune and ordered two lobsters for dinner.

It seemed we were going to be the only fare-paying diners, and our table was set in the empty dining room about as far from the seaplane group, who were in an L near the bar, as you could get. I read nothing in it, but it didn't seem a very positive move in the friendship stakes. I turned to our own business. I was beginning to think that we'd never make Nassau at our present sybaritic rate of progress, so over the lobsters I proposed that we bite off a great chunk of Exumas the next day, some serious sailing, and went all the way up to Hawksbill Cay 25 miles to the north. We could then continue playing there. Just in case the weather turned against us. You shouldn't talk about these things. You shouldn't even mention weather. We left Sampson Cay at 0905, meandered through the channels past Rat and Thomas Cays, Pipe Cay and Compass Cay, and then decided, when we reached Bell Island, that we'd better stop fooling around and sail a straight course. The sky blackened and the first squall came through with 25 knot winds. By the time we passed Cistern Cay, three miles south of Hawksbill, it was clear that there was no question of play time any-where around there. The sea state was building up, as was the wind, and we ploughed on towards Elbow Cay in worsening weather, working out where we could take refuge. Elbow sticks out from the unfortunately named Shroud Cay, and we came close to not making it. By then

I'd started to engines to help us make some progress against the weather, and the port engine alarm came on almost at once, so that was one engine gone. The Tink, which we'd been towing during our gentle, halcyon days was jerking around at the end of her painter like a calf in a rodeo ring, half-filled with water, and we were on near-gale reefing by then. There was only one answer. Make for Norman's Cay, 4 miles to the north, which had a protected central lagoon. We made it. My log seems to have got wet or my pen didn't work too well after our arrival for my last entry reads "Th   God". I dived and checked the anchor, and then stripped and reset the port engine anti-siphon valve. At least we were secure; and we had two engines again.

There was only one other boat in Norman's Cay when we arrived. By nightfall there were sixteen boats there, and next morning another five arrived. The norther continued to blow. None of us were going anywhere for a day. I looked around. It was a curious place with a crashed aircraft, a C-46, awash to window level in the central lagoon and the ruins of a clubhouse complex on the point behind a ruined, sagging jetty. We took the Tink in to the beach to look around, and were joined by about five others. A harassed-looking middle aged woman met us, holding a hand-held radio. One of our fellow refugees, looking equally worried, introduced himself:

" Hi, My name's Richter, like the Scale. We lost our tender, we were towing it, yesterday afternoon. We were about seven miles off, on the Bank. It wouldn't be washed up anywhere near here, would it? Can we contact the Coast Guard? Could I use your radio? I didn't bring my hand-held on shore".

She didn't look too happy and unwillingly parted with her radio while Walter Richter walked round in circles trying to contact a US Coast Guard aircraft. He said he'd seen one fly south just as he was making his way ashore. Amazingly he made contact. Yes, they'd look out for an inflatable. They'd let him know. They had his call sign.

Meanwhile the radio owner was stone-walling friendly questions. Yes, she lived on the island. There was a group of houses, a private development, at the northern tip. Yes, the clubhouse project had failed. Was it the front run by the Colombian drug baron in the 1980s? She didn't know about that. What was the crashed aircraft? She didn't know. She thought it had overshot the runway. Oh, was there still an airport there? No, the runway was closed. No-one was allowed to use it.

More people landed from their boats and children started to run wild, playing on the beach. John and I decided to go back to *Terrapin*, collect our shoes, and go for a walk.

"What do you make of her radio?" I asked him. "You're not allowed to use a marine handheld except on a boat. Why does she want it?"

As we were talking a figure made its way down on to the rocks of the northern point overlooking the beach. There was something awkward about it. I used my binoculars. It was a Bahamian policeman in uniform carrying a rifle down by his side, as if he didn't want the profile of the weapon visible. He settled himself down, laid the rifle on the ground, and spoke briefly into a hand-held radio. Then he picked up a pair of binoculars. I put mine down.

There was little of interest in the ruins of the clubhouse so we walked on to the abandoned airstrip which had great yellow crosses painted across the runway. On the far side, in a group of three houses we'd first taken to be abandoned, there was a Bahamian police detachment base. One of them, half-dressed, came out of the nearest house to ask us who we were, where we'd come from, and made us write our names and home addresses on a page torn from a school exercise book. It seemed a curious form of marine registration, but I've never been reluctant to leave a record of my progress. John was more worried by it. He didn't like it at all. We walked on up the road to the north end of the island, over a ridgeline with a lookout station built out of an old boat on the crest, and on through the remains of a Berlin Wall of concrete blocks which had once, clearly, barred access to the airfield area. We turned back. A twin-engined aircraft passed slowly over the shoreline and returned slowly heading south, almost overhead. The words POLICE were painted under each wing. The engine note changed. It was landing. We approached the airfield cautiously, through the trees at the edge of the road rather than on the road, for the feel of the day justified it. The aircraft was on the ground, its cargo door open. Four or five men, armed with assault rifles were guarding it, looking outwards. One, at least, had a sidearm on his belt. They all wore dark glasses and jeans. The Police detachment were carrying brown boxes out of their house and loading them into the aircraft. It was done as a drill, at some speed. There was no relaxation. No talking.

We faded into the trees and took a long circuit, well away from the airfield, back to the beach. We heard the aircraft take off. Back on *Terrapin* I looked for the sentry overlooking the beach and the anchorage. He was no longer there.

The next day the weather was still lousy. All the captive group of boats stayed put. In the early part of the morning a sentry appeared on the same headland, and some time later we heard an aircraft land. It must have flown in at low level, for we never saw it. About five minutes after it had taken off and left, still unseen, the sentry disappeared. Neither John nor I felt like going ashore, so we spent the day fooling around taking photographs of John in the cockpit of the crashed C-46 for his next Christmas card, and looking for shells on the nearest islet.

John was getting worried. We had 24 hours to get to Nassau. It was only 40 miles to run but the weather was still unkind, still blowing from the north, and we had to cross the Yellow Bank to get to New Providence Island. It had to be a daylight run, with good visibility for the Yellow Bank, both on the chart and in reality, looks as if it had been peppered with coral heads. I promised he'd make it by his check-in time. I listened to the weather report at 0500 the next morning and it was still bad, still on the nose, so I thought, what the hell, we'll motor the shortest route and worked out my courses. The best was 41.85 nm. That would be 8 1/2 hours at something like

5 knots but we'd probably never make that: say 10.46 hours at 4 knots? We set out at 0600.

For eleven hellish hours we slammed into head seas, sometimes making little more than 3 knots. Our average speed came out as 3.8 knots but we made it. We were at the Nassau Yacht Haven by 1715 on Saturday night. I made two resolutions during that awful passage. The first was never again attempt to meet any deadline if the weather was against it, and if deadlines were going to come into the business of sailing, find crew who were free agents or forget the trip. The second resolution was to avoid lonely islands.

It was one year later, in 1993, that an article titled *Sea of Lies* was published in the January 17th edition of the Fort Lauderdale *Sun Sentinel*. It concerned the murder of two Florida sailors, Bill and Patti Kamera, whose yacht *Kalia III* was found by a fellow American boater drifting off Pipe Cay in the Exumas on July 31, 1980. Their boat was a scene of carnage, blood and shattered fiberglass, and their gun-blasted bodies were in the dinghy still secured off *Kalia*'s stern. At least Bill's body was there; a bundled shape, that could have been Patti, was underneath his corpse in the flooded tender. *Kalia III* was later towed into Staniel Cay by a Royal Bahamas Defence Force vessel but there were no bodies when they arrived at the Happy People Marina, just the bloodstained, abandoned yacht with its severed anchor rode. The Bahamian Government refused to take action, for without bodies there was no evidence of violent crime. Admittedly a hunting rifle and the flare gun that were known to have been on board had disappeared, there were three spent flare-pistol cases in the cockpit, the microphone had been ripped from the radio, the radio had been put out of action as well, and the Kamera's cruising cash stock of several thousand dollars was missing. But foul play was ruled out. The United States Government declined to take action. The matter lay outside their jurisdiction. At that time the Colombian drug dealer Carlos Lehder was running Norman's Cay as his private kingdom, and amongst his henchmen was a known killer, a Bahamian called Little Jack; and Little Jack was seen in the 'cigarette' boat, a 30 ft Scarab, he drove for Lehder at Pipe Cay when *Kalia III* was there. It was also known that Lehder had ordered that a sailing boat, which had been off Norman's Cay for several days, should be taken out for it was in the way of a planned drug run. Four men set out in the Scarab to carry out his orders. They returned two hours later with a ripped-out microphone as proof of execution.

The *Kalia* murders are still unsolved today. The killings were never investigated by a government agency. Are the files still open? A 1980 US Congressional Merchant Marine Report stated that "during the last four-year period, 200 US yachts, cabin cruisers and their crews disappeared without a trace on the high seas, most of them in the Caribbean."

TRAVEL SLOWLY TO ARRIVE

Nassau, Bahamas, to Jupiter Inlet, Florida, USA.
March 5 - 18 1992

Terrapin, proud of herself, was wearing all her best flags in celebration when Janet arrived in Nassau, for she'd last seen the little catamaran a thousand miles back in Virgin Gorda which already seemed a long time ago in a very distant country. Other than our ultimate destination which was Jupiter Inlet, two hundred miles away across the Great Bahama Bank and the Gulf Stream, where did Janet want to go? After some guidebook reading she settled for Chub Cay in the Berry Islands, thirty eight miles away across the Providence Channel. We set out at 0700, *Terrapin* still very proud of herself, under her cruising chute. We were off Mamma Rhoda Rock, turning in towards the entrance to the Chub Cay Club Marina channel by lunch time. The passage was over before we'd even settled down. It was a pity that I started the engines a mite too soon for we'd not rehearsed our cruising chute drills and ran over both sheets as we recovered the chute. The cutters on the prop shafts were working perfectly. Years back, in Paris, I'd said that you never knew when they were working; but it's not entirely true. It was not, in truth, the kind of disaster you take to heart for I'd long since decided that the repairs carried out by North Sails in Guadeloupe were less than satisfactory: one of them at the time had described the chute as "a bundle of washing". He was just about right. So we saved the spaghettied sheets for odds and ends, and the

155

chute went back in its bag. At least we were in Chub Cay, and our first little offshore passage was over. With no excitements.

We spent a long weekend there, walking the beaches, searching for conch shells, and looking at the sunsets. It was good, it was perfect, but it was the wrong weekend. Suddenly Chubb Cay Club Marina became utter hell. It was Spring Break. I'd forgotten about that. Four charter boats arrived from Fort Lauderdale, one of them with 31 on board. I never counted the others, but the numbers were around that mark. The partying was non-stop, through the night, and within hours the shore facilities were awash, blocked, ankle deep in litter, and out of order. Nothing worked. Everything was fouled. By Sunday midday we'd had enough. We decided to vote with our feet, leave the party and head across the Bank, undecided at that point whether we'd turn north to Bimini or south to Cat Cay. Much depended on the progress of the Spring Break boats. There must be others out there. Bimini was probably a nightmare. Cat Cay? It was 75 miles to run across the Bank and I wanted to be there in the early evening, if we could make it, so that if we chose to go on, north or south, we'd be entering Cat or Bimini well before midnight. Somehow the fatigue factor seems to increase by 10 after that: out of all proportion to your elapsed out-of-bed time. Psychological fatigue? We could, of course, anchor off Gun Cay light for the night. Anyway, there was no question of attempting a night passage across the Bank, so we sailed at 0600 on Monday.

The crossing was good. We fished and caught a barracuda, threw it back, and caught another. Then I stopped fishing. There was no point. We wouldn't have eaten what we caught, even if it had been a 'good' eating fish, for we were on the reefs and reef fish can be loaded with ciguatera, particularly the predators, the barracudas, snappers, and those big old groupers lurking in their caves. So we went back to sunbathing until the sun went down, and took in the sails as we reached our final waypoint at 2000, just to make life a touch more simple. The weather was good, the wind from the west, and so I motored in towards Gun Cay light and we dropped the anchor when we were well tucked in, well sheltered, in 12 feet of water. I took our anchor bearings and the GPS fix and pasted them up, on Post It notes, in the cockpit under the hardtop.

During the night the wind changed, and just before dawn we were starting to move as it came in from the south east. Spring Break or no, Bimini would be an easy run or we might even think of Honeymoon Harbor, a small cove on the north end of Gun Cay. The starboard engine failed. It was the same trouble I'd had in Norman's Cay with the port engine. Anti-siphon valve. I stripped it and in cleaning the corrosion the valve broke. I had no spare. Brilliant start to the day. OK. Jury rig something. No problem. Then the water pump failed. I couldn't believe it. Impeller? I tried to make Cat Cay on one engine but 20 knots of wind were too much. Turn round. Go to Bimini? I didn't like it all, and turned in to Honeymoon Harbor when we got there. All I wanted at that time was about an hour in sheltered water so that I could carry on with my repairs and get the starboard engine going. Honeymoon was hugger-mugger with Spring Break boats, and my ability to maneuver on one engine in a crowded anchorage was something akin to steering an elephant round an Indian supermarket. We nearly collided with two boats, and despite my appeals for some help, no-one there took any interest. We anchored badly, and started dragging. Nightmare? Yes, it was, for by then the wind was building up and changing to the south west, coming unchecked and straight across the low strip of sand that separates Honeymoon from the Gulf Stream side. Stay there? No way. It was already untenable in my opinion, and it would be a death trap if the wind shifted to the north. If it held for the moment, as a south westerly, we could try for Cat Cay again which was much closer than Bimini. The approach to Bimini, on the Gulf Stream side, would be risky to say the least on one engine. Gun Cay, and then the northern point of Cat Cay itself, would offer some protection as we headed south: all we'd have to contend with would be a bumpy ride as we crossed Gun Cay Channel. And so it proved. We made the Cat Cay Club Marina by mid-afternoon. I don't know about psychological fatigue, but I felt knackered by then. Like Trellis Bay, you could describe it as another sailing adventure, and like Trellis Bay we decided to dine on shore that night. We both needed it; and the pre-dinner drinks. You can underline that final 's'.

By the next morning the wind had shifted to the north west and was constant at 26-28 knots. There was no question of going anywhere. I had my repairs to carry out, and no-one in their right mind would attempt to cross the Gulf Stream with wind against current. We stayed put. I thought we might have to wait it out for 48 hours. We were there for six days. As Janet said, you get to know a place well over six days, perhaps better than you intended, if it's only two miles long and barely a mile wide. If it were some consolation, we'd heard that Bimini was like a scene from a Hieronymous Bosch painting with Spring Break charter boats, a fishing competition, and refugees from Honeymoon Harbor vying for every inch of space. The isolation of Cat Cay was not to be regretted. One of the Spring Break boats from Chub Cay put in briefly on Day 2, on their way back to Lauderdale, and set off again after two hours. I thought they were crazy and I thought the captain should have had his licence withdrawn: I was certain that he hadn't enough life jackets and the life raft capacity to cover everyone on board. Janet, talking to one teenager, was told that there weren't enough berths for them all so they shared, and, of course, used the berths of those who were on watch. She herself had no foul weather gear, just a sweatshirt. It was her first time at sea, and most of them were pathetically ill-equipped for anything other than a day cruise along the Intercoastal Waterway. The charter captain wouldn't talk of the weather and the effect of the norther on the Gulf Stream. His charter ended that day and he was getting back. Janet returned to *Terrapin* and lent her new friend a set of our oilskins.

She wrote from her college returning them later. Their passage back to Lauderdale had been hell. Everyone was sick; and scared to death. She would never sail again.

There was some advantage in being so close to Florida. I had some spares I needed flown in on the Cat Cay aircraft, so by the weekend we were in good shape with new anti-siphon valves, new cooling hoses, and new water pump impellers on both engines. But on Monday it was still the same story, winds NW-N-NE. Never less than 20 knots, No-Go. If there was a momentary break, I told Janet, we'd go for it like rattlesnakes. The passage planning was long since ready, in the log, with all the tides worked out, for the tide state would be critical as we approached Jupiter Inlet. It was 99.5 nm to my chosen waypoint off the Inlet, and a two mile run-in. We'd be going across the Gulf Stream in a great gentle curve, letting ourselves be taken north past all the boltholes we could use in an emergency: Port Everglades, Hillsboro Inlet, Boca, Boynton, and Lake Worth. We talked and we read and we walked and we waited.

The break came on Tuesday afternoon. The wind had switched to the east, 15-20 knots, with seas forecast in the Gulf Stream at 3-5 ft, and we had a full moon. What else could you ask for? That was it.

The rattlesnaking started. We sailed at 1955 and were off Gun Light by 2018. The timings mattered, every minute counted. Then the great curve started, *Terrapin* sailing beautifully with a bone in her teeth and her rudders biting deep, well hunkered down to her business, and the lights and the silhouettes of ship after ship fell astern of us to north and to south. It was bumpy out there, but then we were moving, not fooling around. You don't ease off in the rattlesnake business. You go to broad timings, marking the chart every hour, and keep sailing. We were off Lauderdale by 0200, Pampano at 0300, Boca at 0400, Delray at 0500, Lake Worth at 0600, Palm Beach at 0700, and Riviera Beach at 0800. First light had come and we'd seen the white condos of Delray flush with the pink of dawn, and between Lake Worth and Palm Beach an early morning flight of pelicans came slowly past in line astern at cross-tree height. Welcoming us, Janet said. By then she was sitting on the forward edge of the foredeck, snugged up against the pulpit, her bare feet kissing the water each time *Terrapin* dipped in the wave troughs. There was a sudden shout:

"Porpoises. Oh look, it's porpoises. They've come to welcome us too" and there they were, seven or eight of them, racing each other and crisscrossing ahead of *Terrapin*'s bows, falling back and urging us forward again. Certain that we knew where we going, they left us off Juno Beach when we started to angle closer to the shore, and then there was another shout :

"Oh Boo, I can't believe it. A turtle. Welcoming us too. It's too much".

Janet turned with tears in her eyes, and off the port bow a great loggerhead turtle raised its head to watch us pass, totally unworried by *Terrapin*. That kind of thing can unhinge you; but by then we had the red column of Jupiter lighthouse in view and we were right on the mark at high tide. It was like getting three lemons on a slot machine. The Florida inlets are potentially hazardous and claim lives every year, for in almost every case you have a witch's brew of Atlantic waves and onshore winds piling up against shoal waters, sand bars, and river flow and, if you get everything wrong, an ebb tide. Rather than winning a silver stream of quarters from our slot machine that morning, we had the sailor's dream: full water, slack tide, just the Loxahatchee running against us, and more than enough punch with wind and wave behind us to counter the river's flow. We surfed into the Inlet so fast I thought "you've blown it, you've blown it, you're going to lose control" and then suddenly we were in calmer water. Sails down. Report in. Get cleared. We motored to the reporting dock. One telephone call on the direct line to the US Coast Guard. Record the clearance number in the log. Then we turned with the ebb tide, passed the lighthouse again, and made another turn to the north into the Intercoastal Waterway. I called the Jupiter Island bridgekeeper as I made my turn to say that I didn't need the bridge to be opened, for the southern bridge to the island comes up immediately. I was turning into the Jib Club Marina. It was there, almost under the bridge, to starboard.

We were turning, even then, and within minutes we were easing *Terrapin*'s 26 feet gently into the berth that had long been allocated to us, barely making way, and she had lost all movement as her fenders just kissed the decking. I looked at my watch after I'd switched off the engines. It was 1000 in the morning on Wednesday March 18th 1992. Right on the hour. Suddenly it was quiet, there seemed to be no noise, just the fluttering of *Terrapin*'s flags in the east wind, her new ensign on the starboard backstay (for the original one had long been shredded by the winds) and her faded house flag at the cross-trees.

"*Terrapin. Terrapin*, Little One, we've made it. You're home now. We've made it home."

164

AFTERNOTE

Terrapin was unaffected by Hurricane Andrew in August 1992, for she was tucked safely up the St Lucie River, over a hundred miles from Biscayne Bay and Homestead. If the storm had veered north in its final approach to Florida, as is so often the case with hurricanes, and if its track had passed over Stuart, I don't think any of the boats there would have survived despite being eight miles inland from the ocean, with an offshore island, a strip of coast, and the St Lucie River to absorb the tidal surge. The wind would have done the damage. But who can guess about these things?

Nine months after my return I was asked whether I would sell *Terrapin*. The answer was an immediate 'no'. I still had islands to visit and blue water to cross. Our journeying was by no means over. Then, on reflection, my conclusion changed to a qualified 'yes'. It sounds traitorously disloyal, more so when I say that nothing has brought my love affair to an end. Let me explain. *Terrapin* and I are sailing now and may sail on for years yet, but we've reached the end of the tracks I first drew on my charts four years ago, and we've reached the end of our development curves: *Terrapin* is in top shape. Beyond doubt the best of her kind. Yes, the part-rational, part-irrational love of Man for boat remains, but I would be untruthful if I didn't admit to entertaining new ideas, possibilities and projections I never first considered; and, with this, inevitably, go thoughts about the design of another boat, for you should always try to match horses to courses. What else do you think about during the hours you are on watch? It's the endemic preoccupation of those who set out to sea. Nothing is constant but change. I remind myself that my Phoenician captain would never have made it across the Atlantic if he hadn't kept reaching out, time and time again, far beyond the horizons of the world in which he first found himself.

That brings us to an introspective personal assessment of the effect that the three years I spent taking *Terrapin* home to Jupiter Inlet has had on me. Read no further, if you wish, for this book is NOT an ego trip. I like to think that it has made me a better person, a more gentle person, but only Janet and my friends can judge that. I don't believe, I never have believed, in the conventional character improving schemes, sailing before the mast around the Horn, or enduring outlandish Outward Bound survival exercises, but maybe *Terrapin*, or the little onyx terrapin, taught me something. I reassure myself that the gentleness, in a world which is still far too brutal, is not debilitating. What else? It has confirmed my long-held conviction that the great early American civilizations owed everything, other than their labor force, to the Mediterranean. It has made me much more aware, and much more concerned, about the future of this planet; and I thought, long before I started on my voyaging, that I was in the forefront of the Greens. I fear terribly, now, the effects of overpopulation. We are on the point of crisis. Overburdened with people. Looking at it as a sailor, we are fished out, poisoning our oceans, and killing our reefs. The planet will survive in some mutated way. Will our great-grandchildren enjoy living in the world we are handing on to them? I cannot conclude that they will bless us for their inheritance.

Turning from my epochal scale and returning to affairs within the reach of human hands, Nikki, Phil, and I have remained in touch and exchange news. In 1993 they took *Two Minds* back to England from the Mediterranean, after a series of seasonal voyages that came close to rivalling the travels of Jason's *Argo*, sold *Two Minds*, and are now rebuilding their resources to buy another boat and set out again. Without wallowing in self-analysis, I feel an enduring kinship with them, a bonding that I can only describe as being 'veteran-like', and at times I wonder about the stress and tensions that are the inevitable by-product of attempting to take a small craft, just 22 ft on the waterline, across the North Atlantic. I could handle it better today. What else did I learn? I now have the most profound respect for the forces of Nature. The power of wind and wave, and the way in which weather can change suddenly, are something that none of us should ever underrate. If you set out into the seas and oceans of the world, you get your part of the preparation right; but you still go hand in hand with your Maker.

Alice went to a sailing school in Florida in December 1992, and in April and May 1993 she and I, with two other friends, took *Terrapin* to the Bahamas to cruise in the Abacos. Janet and I covered much the same route earlier this year. As fate had it, after an idyllic start in the fair weather forecast by every authority, our passage back to the islands over the Gulf Stream turned into an endurance run as a result of the freak unseen coincidence of a triangle of three Lows framing the Florida Strait. It was our worst offshore passage ever, a night of chaotic triangular waves and violent motion. By dawn we had hit our limits, and we'd had all the additional character building we could take. I can't think how we made it to West End, Grand Bahama: but it was *Terrapin* who won through. Or perhaps the real star was the little onyx terrapin, still safe in her Vermont cherry frame between the two forward windows in the saloon, where she had always been since the start.

In setting off in your dreamboat on your dream voyage, you come back time and again to the Paulik Lazishkin philosophy. 'Nobody knows what will be tomorrow...'

    Jupiter Island
    June 1994   MW

ACCUMULATED WISDOM
AND
REFITS AND RETHINKS

ACCUMULATED WISDOM

In my childhood any book worth reading used to be laced with advice, exhortations, and encouragement to the reader. I've never felt inclined to follow suit, or missed the practice when it fell out of conventional favor, for in truth it turned me off. I thought it patronizing.

Now I eat my hat. I change tack. You may put this book aside at this point, for *Terrapin* and I have told our story, unless you really want to plough on through her tool kit and my medical pack; but for those who may be at the beginning of their learning curve, as I was, some of my data may be useful. Why start with a blank slate unless you have to? My addendum, if you can call it that, is the kind of miscellany I would have liked to have at hand before I started. What follows is an assessment of *Terrapin*, and, in broad terms, some of the basic requirements for an ocean sailing craft. Thereafter lists follow, dull lists!, their succession broken only by one brief comment on learning to sail *Terrapin*. This apart, it is list after list, and none of them are compulsory reading. My only guarantee is that they are the checklists I've used, and built up, over five years. Call them my accumulated wisdom, if you like.

But be warned: there may be terrible loopholes in them and many things I've overlooked. Give me another five years and they might be better. In the meantime, they may help someone, sometime. I hope so.

REFITS AND RETHINKS

It's a truism to say that the state of your boat is vital, but I use this as a lead-in to what may seem a negative approach. What went wrong with *Terrapin*? Much of it has come out in my story so I won't expand on it. At the start let me just flick over the pages of your memory bank. My notes and my remarks cover my experience with *Terrapin* over two years from March 1990 to March 1992. During this time *Terrapin* sailed 7,267.22 nm from Birdham Pool, England, to Jupiter Inlet, Florida, and logged a number of miles, which I've not included in my total, cruising in the British Virgin Islands. Air temperatures ranged from below freezing in Northern France to 98°F in the West Indies. Wind states ranged from flat calm to Force 8 (with touches of 9) and the sea state, at its worst, was 15 ft swells with contrary 4-6 ft wind-driven waves superimposed on the swell. My longest continuous open water passage was 2,011 nm from Porto Grande, São Vicente, Cape Verde Islands, to Barbados which took 17.5 days at an average speed of 4.78 knots.

I said that my two greatest irritants were electrics and my sprayhood-bimini, and so it was. The distribution panel for a boat, even a sail boat, must be state of the art, well-laid out, and accessible. All wiring must be color-coded and labelled; all wiring runs should be laid in conduits with ample space left for additional runs and leaders left ready for use. Provision should be made that all spare bulbs, fuses, and circuit breakers are stored in a specially built locker by the panel. I's my impression that the UK is a quarter of a century behind the rest of the western world in its approach to marine electrics. I hope

173

I'm wrong; but I fear, even now, that someone is building a boat that will get it all wrong at the start. What about minor electrical failures? The masthead tricolor bulb worked itself loose. Rough weather prevented any action to make it good at sea. Three fluorescent tubes failed and one reading light bulb. I mentioned the subminiature indicator lights in the main control panel. As for the AC hookup nonsense, it was my fault. The circuit diagram I gave *Terrapin*'s builder was not clear enough. I wanted to include an automatic transfer switch: we built-in a total cut-off. It would be logical, having spoken of electrics, to move straight on to electronics. The Autohelm 4000 failed in mid-Atlantic. Part of the cause was salt water contamination, and part due to a stretched drive belt. The speed/log Autohelm ST-50 transducer failed on leaving the Canaries. It is a sealed unit and had to be replaced in Barbados. GPS, as it was, provided a far more accurate means of navigation across the Atlantic, but it was more than irritating to lose one means of fixing position. Celestial navigation became my only backup to GPS. Next time I would carry a spare transducer.

Turning to my other area of primary dissatisfaction, canvas sprayhoods are an anachronism, particularly in a boat which has no interior wheel station. This must be even more true for a boat where the majority of its kind, by geographic distribution, are sailing in cold waters, wind, and rain much of the time. I went through two sprayhoods and two biminis, neither of which were satisfactory in use, and both deteriorated to the point where not only did they fail to serve their primary function, but the lines of the boat were spoilt by ill-fitting canvas. I recommend designing boats at the outset with GRP cockpit shielding. Surely the He-Man business of taking spray in your face went out with the Vikings? My boom gallows, with its linking bimini (and don't forget the zip-on side curtains) running forward to the hardtop, is an integral part of my cockpit protection package. I'll say no more.

What about other faults? Let's turn to sails, running rigging, and the like. My cruising chute failure, when the head strop parted, was nothing but a one-off accident. A substandard eye pressing. Let's forget that. The roller reefing forestay head swivel partially jammed at sea due to salt build up. I'll say at once that I'd not kept it washed clean with fresh water as it should have been; but Teflon spray and some precious water put it right. It was almost impossible to work on it in the open ocean. The original mooring lines just lasted the voyage but replacements, in the interests of safety, had to be bought half way through the trip; and the mainsail tack shackle failed. The main anchor needed beefing up with that extra 30 ft of 5/16ths chain, for 20 ft of chain is not enough. I speak with the experience of enduring Force 7 winds in the supposedly idyllic anchorages of São Vicente and the Îles des Saintes, and similarly marginal conditions, suffered not by choice, elsewhere. It is bound to happen on an extended cruise. Ask me now where I spent most of my time? I'd say much of my two years at sea was spent either in the engine compartments or upside down in the heads. Let's start with the engines. Anti-siphon valves must be saltwater corrosion proof. Heaven knows where my original ones came from, but they appeared to have been designed for anything other than a marine environment and gave me continuous trouble right from the start, initially spraying the new engines with salt water to the point where instant corrosion of both engine and mounting bolts set in. Later, after endless experiment, a network of aquarium plastic piping had the spray problem under control, but the valves themselves failed in the end. It was simple enough in Florida to fit new anti-siphon loops without my network of aquarium plastic piping, much improved, fail-safe, draining through the outer hulls so that you had a visual indication that the system was working. And with Vieques Sound in my mind, I had the exhausts rerun to vent further aft and the exhaust waterlocks changed for better. Were there any other engine problems? One engine backfired and blew out its air filter. I never discovered why. Thereafter it used fractionally more oil than its twin, but gave no more trouble. One engine developed a salt water leak when the seal in its water cooling pump failed. It was one spare I didn't carry at the start. The leak was not critical and was later fixed without difficulty. The port engine ignition switch failed due to salt water corrosion, and it too was easily made good again. Of course there were those impeller failures. But impellers do fail. The answer is preventive maintenance. Change them regularly.

I think the Heavenly Twins 27 is under-engined with Yanmar 1GM10 9 hp diesels. Its standard fit should be 2GM20 18 hp engines so that you can make useful and safe progress, rather than struggle, against tide rips and through wind acceleration zones. The weight penalty, 35lbs extra for each engine, is minimal. But I'm not a yacht designer and the more powerful engines would probably result in terrible side-effects like digging the stern under. My point is, I guess, that if you have engine options, go for the one with the greatest punch. Having stepped outside my expertise, I'd better go back to familiar territory and hang upside down in the heads. The macerator pump failed, jammed through misuse. I replaced it later with a manual pump, in pursuit of a simpler life and to cut down demands for 12V power. The manual pump failed when a piston clip broke. I had no spare, and had to make a replacement out of soft wire, which miraculously stayed working for weeks. *Terrapin* has now cornered the market in toilet spares and we may well have caused a worldwide shortage of PAR parts. We're ready for anything, electric or manual. And I still have my bucket.

Let's stay with water systems for a while, and look at taking water where you want it. Far too many of the plastic hose clips on my pressurized water pipelines failed and I replaced them all with stainless steel clips. Double clips. Never accept plastic; and ensure that every single one of your through-hull fittings, above and below the waterline, are double-clipped. Some of mine were not. One Whale hand pump was defective (it had a hairline crack in it) and had to be replaced. Two Whale micro switches in the pressurized system failed early in their life and had to be replaced. Now let's turn to suffering from water where you don't want it. One solar vent leaked. Its sealing mastic had not been correctly applied. The steering arm gaiters leaked. This could have been anticipated and prevented during the build.

Later the original gaiters cracked under the cumulative effect of wear and sunlight. The console and the cockpit suffered recurrent flooding upwards through the cockpit drains, as did the cockpit sole locker (which was more than half filled with water much of the time in the early stages of the voyage), and similarly the two foredeck lockers, and the sinks in the galley and the heads all suffered from slamming-induced surge flooding, jets of water forced up the drains. It was easily solved: fit deflectors over the through-hull exits, and an additional gate ball valve on the cockpit sole locker drain. Conventional non-return valves are useless. They become jammed with debris. I used clam shell shields in the Virgin Island refit, but later, in Florida, had to make a more professional job of it. One problem couldn't be solved until Florida. The polycarbonate windows in the saloon and the aft cabin had creeping leaks, almost from the outset. Why? Poor seating; and the effect of stress and flexing. They were not through-bolted. Beware of large areas of plastic. Big windows look good in port; but old-fashioned portholes would be better at sea.

On interior design, I soon found that the galley stove should have been set back fractionally with a safety rail running in front of the control knobs, in line with the galley counter front, to prevent anyone brushing or falling against the controls, which happened more than once at sea. After some thought I decided too that the stove should be mounted on sliding rails so that it could be slid out to clean around its base, and so that anything dropped between the stove and the work top could be recovered easily. This conversion can be achieved relatively simply: two sections of mast track and sliders will do it. But the tracking must be lockable. On lighting I had one late, blinding glimpse of the obvious. I had two separate circuits: white light and red light. It would have been simpler to fit dual white-red fluorescent lights everywhere, and keep the reading lights on the same circuit. Then you would have your red light option for passage-making, and, when you were tucked up in your berth, you could still use your white tulip light for reading. Keep it simple?

As I close my 'faults' list, I should add that to my surprise I found it necessary to dive under *Terrapin* every 3-4 weeks, green pot scourer in hand, otherwise the weed, goose barnacles, and coral worm triumphed in establishing an impressively mature submarine garden. I had thought that a blitz every eight weeks might be the norm for remedial cleaning, but it was not so. Does CopperClad work? Yes, way better than anti-fouling. But if you put it on your hulls, your pot scourer days are far from done. Hardly a fault, you might say. I mention it only as a caution.

In Florida two things became clear soon after my arrival. The first was that *Terrapin* couldn't spend the hurricane months in the Jib Club Marina unless I was there to take her to a hurricane hole whenever a storm threatened. I wouldn't be there; I couldn't be there, full time. The answer was to take *Terrapin* somewhere offering greater protection over the critical months. And refit at the same time? Stuart Yacht? Up the St Lucie River? It was an inspired choice. Gregg Burdick and Doug Newbigin were into catamarans. Doug had designed, built, and sailed his own across the Atlantic taking almost exactly the course I had chosen. We talked. My list seemed endless; but like a major service on your car, despite the shock when the bill comes in, these things have to be done. What then were my priorities?

Shall we talk about safety first? It was not just the memory of the Caicos Bank or the Yellow Bank that made me do this, or a return to that primal cruising fear of collision, but I wanted to be as sure as I could be that *Terrapin* would survive hitting a coral head or that mythical floating container. She already had sealed air compartments in each bow. I had them foam-filled, foam-filled the forward half of each keel, put substantial reinforcement over and around the leading edges of each keel, and fitted two additional automatic bilge pumps. Turning to less traumatic fears, I replaced all plastic through-hull fittings with bronze fittings, fitted new lifelines, improved the emergency steering, and fitted an electronic barometer/weather station. I reckon you need really accurate warning of weather changes when you're out there. An ordinary pretty-looking brass marine barometer is not enough. Then I set about designing the fourth version of my MOB equipment 'package'. The first three had failed every test and it seemed that the problems of mounting a Danbuoy, a horseshoe lifebuoy, and a strobe light so that all three, linked together, could be deployed instantly from a centre cockpit, without failure, were beyond the wit of Man (myself included in that humanity). I think I've got it right now. As I complained early in my voyaging, the horseshoe lifebuoy originally fitted on *Terrapin*, made by an Italian firm, was the stuff of lawsuits (it was part of the first MOB rig which failed so dismally in the Mar Menor on the Costa Blanca). The loops securing the lifebuoy to its encircling polypropylene line were secured only by single mild steel staples. Nothing else. Similarly the same firm's self-activating light failed through the penetration of salt corrosion after only eight days at sea. It was also useless as a light. Nothing but a flashlight bulb which would never have been visible in rough seas. You must have a strobe, the most powerful one you can find. Don't buy cheap stuff. Unless you value life in nickels and dimes.

The dreaded electrics came next. There was just one simple task: get rid of all through-deck fittings. Run the wind generator cord and the antenna coax for the SSB radio through the deck to dry connections far inside the hull. Run the masthead cables, all of them, wind instruments, radio, GPS, and lights into a conduit leading upwards inside the hardtop to a terminal bar inside a watertight box; and then take the new cabling down through the coachroof in another conduit. Label the terminals inside the lid of the watertight box. Pack the entry and exit conduits with silicone sealant. Spray LPS 3 inside the watertight box. Corrosion problem over. Ended. We then turned to motive power. The engines. And then the sails and replaced all chafed running rigging. It was necessary. It remained was to look at comfort. Replace the saloon and aft cabin plexiglass windows with through-bolted Lexan. Replace the flexible water tanks, which had torn from their fastening straps in the pounding of head seas, with aluminum tanks with gauges. And design the ultimate version of those slamming surge deflectors over all the through-hull drains.

In a nutshell, that was it. Of course there were half-a-hundred other things requiring attention, and things which had required attention during my passage-making, but it would be tedious to list them. What I'm trying to do is give a feel for the attrition of two years at sea, and the bull points to consider, in design, before you set out. It may seem that my message is one of nothing but gloom and dollar signs, but, as I said at the start, I think you have to start with the negatives. The fundamental plus point is that *Terrapin* made it across the Atlantic in a year that was reckoned to be marked by unusual and unseasonable high winds and high seas. The same abnormal conditions applied in the Caribbean, where although the lee of the islands themselves offered sheltered water, the inter-island gaps were, almost without exception, brutal passages.

What I would single out as vital equipment on *Terrapin*, equipment without which I would not attempt a similar passage on any boat, are:

autopilot (Autohelm 4000)
GPS
SSB radio
mast steps (for repair work and eyeball navigation)
U bolt for safety harness in the cockpit
jacklines
helmsman's seat (for comfort)
swimming ladder (for convenience)

These 'extras' were worth their weight in gold. Perhaps I should add that a good tool kit and every conceivable spare you can muster is the best preventive treatment I know to keep the rats of worry, which can breed on a long passage, at bay. But this is obvious.

It remains to reflect on four lines of thought that have been much on my mind in the last year. The first is the absurdity of the Pentagon's degradation of the GPS signal available to civilian users, the reimposition of Selective Availability, on the grounds that national security demands it. This deliberate distortion of GPS signals was originally intended to deny the system to the Soviets. It was a false premise, even then. In the Gulf War SA was waived totally. Who now is our enemy? Why should I die on a reef because some military bureaucrat in Northern Virginia has not looked out of his window in ten years? After the GPS system had been developed and advertised as the best news for the yachting world since long-life milk, I believe the US Government has a moral responsibility to deliver the goods. In full measure. The Pentagon's reimposition of SA is even more absurd now that the requirements of the US Coast Guard and the technology of the GPS receiver-makers has led to the development of the unclassified differential capability, which will give us a greater positional accuracy than we all achieved when SA was off. But this system, based on the augmentation of GPS by radio signals broadcast from land, is unlikely to become worldwide; and the target date for its introduction in US coastal waters to serve most US harbors is 1996. Why should we be forced to upgrade our existing GPS receivers, despite the very limited geographic coverage of DGPS, just to gain its significant advantages in some difficult approaches? What kind of difference in accuracy are we taking about? GPS with SA in force will give your position to about 300 ft. DGPS, working through SA, will give you a fix to 30 ft. But let's look at the world as a whole, not just coming into Boston or San Francisco in fog. We're not playing around out there: in foul weather, and in the blackness of night, we need accuracy, not just to avoid rocks (for the charts might be wrong) but to assess our drift, the force of currents, to know exactly what progress we are making. On my return, all too conscious that my Sand Bore Channel passage would have been a touch more relaxing with GPS, I wrote to two Senators and two Congressmen. The replies I got were identical handouts. What you might call a knee-jerk *apparatchik* reaction from the Pentagon. My initial question "Why SA?" remains unanswered.

What about weather? Have the world's weather patterns really altered? I read my Pilot Charts, the predictions of winds, wave heights, gales, tropical cyclones, ocean currents, air and sea surface temperatures, surface pressure, visibility, and ice limits for every month of the year, collated since recording first began in the last century. All I can say is that nothing measured. Maybe 1991 was exceptional, but I'm left with the gut conviction that winds are stronger, and the winter 'Christmas Wind' period longer, than the predictions would have you believe. In short, yes. I think we've fouled it up. Just the same way that we've fouled up the ocean that is the Mother-Source of this planet. You see the effects and the marks of pollution everywhere you sail. I do not like to be depressive. I loathe being cast in the role of a prophet of doom. But if you live in a good, suburban, sanitized environment, with recycling going satisfactorily, get out there and sail an ocean. See how the world is really shaping. And then come back and tell your children about it. Tell them about the world they will really inherit.

I express concern about the environment but in my own obsessions I'll admit at once to one paradox: I prefer plastic to glass. I dislike having glass on *Terrapin*. I use plastic 'glasses' and minimize the glass jars and bottles I take on board. My fear is simply broken glass. I don't dump my plastic at sea. Not even my empty water bottles, space-eating though they are, for I always carry packs of bottled water to supplement my tanks. Any other signs of paranoia or psychosis? Yes. I can't stand smoking. I used to smoke once myself; and I suppose the converted to any faith are always the fanatics. I have a passion for tidyness. I must be able to lay my hands on everything in the boat, no matter what it is or where it may be, in the dark; or, if you want the ultimate disaster scenario, even if I have to dive under and work my way into the capsized boat. At sea I keep a scuba tank hooked up to my regulator and BC, with a mask, in the outboard starboard dive tank rack in the cockpit, just in case. In the early days when at last I'd worked out my stowage plan, I used to lie in my berth, close my eyes, and play Kim's Game (read Kipling's *Kim*, the story of an Indian boy whose powers of memory were trained in games to serve his master in espionage). Night after night I made my way foot by foot from stem to stern, mentally listing everything that was there. I could do the dive-in-the-dark act for real, but I hope I never have to try it. My confession ends with the conviction that navigation should be carried out on shore or in harbor. Everything should be worked out before you sail, not just where you're going and how you think you'll get there, but every alternative, all your waypoints, with time and space calculations for a broad span of different speeds of advance, and if you're making a landfall, everything step by step, just as you'll need it, from lights to tides to bridge opening times. Remember my Sand Bore Channel nonsense? I broke that rule then. You can take decisions while you're under way but you shouldn't saddle yourself with the grunt work of basic navigation. Not at sea. It takes you away from the novel you've always wanted to read; or you might get a lungful of diesel and not feel wildly enthusiastic about desk work.

What of sailing in the future? Navigation is certainly going to be easier as GPS becomes the standard worldwide system and GPS receivers become cheap enough so that we can all afford battery powered backup sets. Your sextant really will belong in a maritime museum then. The SSB radio is on the way out. We'll get a satellite telephone system going that will allow you to take your personal telephone number with you wherever you go. Think of the safety factor in that, when all you've got to do is punch numbers to get through with crystal clarity and you can read your position instantly off your GPS. I think low-demand low-drain electronics are going to bring our power problems to an end too (I speak as a sailor), and that will be good. If there's any change I would wish for, but I see no sign of it coming yet, it is to move into the 21st Century in the matter of lights. We seem stuck in a 19th Century quagmire of using red, green, and white, as the basic colors of the seagoing light system. Yes, of course some exceptions have crept in, the occasional daring use of yellow, but look at the Navigation Rules and turn to Lights and Shapes. Can you remember the awful dreary business of learning all the confusion of greens on reds on whites so that you could pass your first exam? Next time you're flying at night, look out of the window as you land. Note the way high intensity lighting every color of the rainbow marks the runways, taxiways, apron areas; all the complexity of an airport. Why don't us seafarers make use of every color known to Man, and make use of strobes too? If IATA, or whoever controls such things, can achieve it, surely the IMO or our guardian organization can? The need for lights will be always with us.

Enough. Let me turn to the 'dull lists' I promised. If they seem basic, kindergarten, stuff just reflect that human memory is fallible, particularly under conditions of fatigue or stress. No aircraft pilot takes-off or lands without going through a check list. Why not play it safe at sea? You don't have to play everything as a drill if you have a hang-up about individual freedom and liberty, but your first time crew might appreciate an aide-memoir. As I've never been keen on writing myself the same list of reminders time and time again, bit by bit I've put myself together a 'Fool's Guide' to the routine business of going to sea, lest one day I suffer a chronic attack of amnesia. The result is a folder that you could call *Terrapin*'s 'bible'. The following pages are a part of it.

CHECKLISTS

PUTTING OUT TO SEA

fill diesel tanks, propane tanks, and outboard fuel tank
check reserve oil and lubricants
fill water tanks
take bottled water [minimum on passage 2 liters per person per day]
ice? ice block in cold box?
prepare first day/night on-passage food

check all survival equipment including emergency water jerricans
check man overboard equipment: strobe light OK?
check engine oil levels; bilges dry; nav lights, spotlight, spreaders, all interior lights working
check stores: fully provisioned and stores listed? [3 x passage time x hands ÷ 2]
check nav kit list
nav work completed:
>   waypoints
>   courses, times and distances: alternatives if bad weather?
>   lights listed and tides known
>   weather forecast checked
>   nav watches and clock checked with UT
check ship's papers complete: documentation; FCC licence; insurance
courtesy flag for next port?
check crew passports OK: open log and list crew

stow for rough weather and clear decks
rig jacklines and check harnesses
garbage ashore
port authority departure clearances?
inform someone of route and destination?

radios and nav instruments on
secure open lights and hatches
headcount before sailing
new crew safety briefing including MOB drills and
Abandoning Ship responsibilities

WATCHKEEPING

Crew of 2

0600-0800	social	both up
0800-1300	A	5 hrs
1300-1800	B	5 hrs
1800-2000	social	both up
2000-2300	A	3 hrs
2300-0200	B	3 hrs
0200-0400	A	2 hrs
0400-0600	B	2 hrs

Crew of 3

0001-0400	A	all watches 4 hrs
0400-0800	B	
0800-1200	C	
1200-1600	A	
1600-2000	B	all up social 1800-2000
2000-2359	C	

skipper is normally C and is on call during other watches.
rotate weekly on long passages

Crew of 4

0001-0600	A B	one of the two can catnap
0600-1200	C D	
1200-1800	A B	all up social 1800-2000
1800-2359	C D	one of the two can catnap

skipper is normally in CD slot
if three watchkeepers and 1 cook, watchkeepers work on
timings for a crew of 3

TERRAPIN LOG [I found the GPS/Met log worked well for me. The rest is straightforward]

DATE_____ FROM _____ TO _____

crew _____ _____ _____

_____ _____ _____

BOAT STATE AT START

port engine hours	_____	port engine battery	[1]	_____
starboard engine hours	_____	starboard engine battery	[2]	_____
fuel port engine	_____	house batteries	[3]	_____
fuel starboard engine	_____	water port tank ____ stb ____ cans ____		

WAYPOINTS AND COURSE [add more legs if you need them]

leg	from	position	course °M	distance to run	
1	_____	_____	_____	_____	to 2
2	_____	_____	_____	_____	to 3
3	_____	_____	_____	_____	to 4
4	_____	_____	_____	_____	to 5
5	_____	_____	_____	_____	to 6
6	_____	_____	_____	_____	to dest
destination	_____		total distance to run	_____	

TIDES

departure point	HW	_____ _____	destination	HW	_____ _____
	LW	_____ _____		LW	_____ _____

WEATHER FORECAST

REFERENCE CHARTS

GPS/MET LOG [GPS sequence based on a Magellan]

TIME						
position						
GQ/SQ						
course steered						
course required						
distance to run						
XTE						
correction						
speed						
DMG						
barometer						
wind						

NOTES

distance run this 24 hrs _____

date _____ _____ signatu

COMING INTO PORT

approach chart?
land contours and features
coastal pilot?
harbor chart?
harbor signals? any special timings: bridges or the like?
VHF channel?
state of tide and tidal stream?
local wind pattern?
list navigation aids in order of likely utility: lights; marks;
bottom contours and depths

location of reporting dock
fly courtesy flag and Q flag
prepare anchor; fenders; and lines
harbor chart; VHF; binoculars; compass; loud hailer;
whistle and air horn on hand

nav instruments stay on until log data recorded
arrival clearances: ship's papers
write up log
check bilges and check engines. top up engine oil
garbage ashore
fill water and fuel tanks
washing and laundry
swab down decks

security if leaving boat: one person to stay on board?
security of tender and outboard if left unattended in port
or on beach?

DISTRESS CALL

[SSB RADIO 2182 kHZ and VHF CHANNEL 16]

HELLO ALL SHIPS: MAYDAY: MAYDAY: MAYDAY

THIS IS YACHT   [name]_____   [callsign]_____
THIS IS YACHT   [name]_____   [callsign]_____
THIS IS YACHT   [name]_____   [callsign]_____

MAYDAY: THIS IS   [name]_____   [callsign]_____

OUR POSITION IS _____

WE ARE _____
[state the emergency: on fire, sinking after hitting an object: whatever is life threatening]
WE REQUIRE IMMEDIATE ASSISTANCE _____
[explain exactly what: rescue because of abandoning ship; a tow having stayed on the hull]

WE HAVE _____ PERSONS ON BOARD

AT THIS TIME WE ARE _____
[describe the action being taken: preparing to take to the liferaft; or remaining on board]

FOR IDENTIFICATION WE ARE A [type of boat, length, color of hull] AND OUR LIFERAFT HAS [color] CANOPY. WE HAVE A 121 POINT 5 MEGAHERTZ EPIRB [if this applies] [or a 406 MEGAHERTZ EPIRB if applicable], AND [if this applies] WE HAVE FLARES AND SMOKE SIGNALS, OCEAN DYE MARKERS, AND A HAND-HELD VHF RADIO. WE WILL KEEP LISTENING WATCH ON 2182 AND CHANNEL 16 AS LONG AS WE CAN.

THIS IS YACHT   [name] _____   [callsign] _____
MAYDAY OVER
[repeat message until an acknowledgment is received]

ABANDONING SHIP

Each member of the crew <u>must have the specific responsibility</u> for taking one or more of the actions listed below:

1. <u>THE LIFERAFT</u>
   ensure the liferaft is fully fitted and ready to go: keep on deck <u>until orders given</u> to launch; and after launch keep painter secured to boat <u>until orders given</u> to cast off.

2. <u>EMERGENCY SURVIVAL PACKS</u> [for contents of Packs see Commissioning List]
   lash all emergency packs [orange waterproof boxes containing food and essential equipment] to a lifebuoy or flotation device so that the survival pack boxes can be thrown into the water <u>on orders</u> having first been secured to the liferaft.
   [emergency packs will not be taken on board the liferaft until after abandoning ship]

3. <u>EMERGENCY WATER CANS</u>
   lash all 2 gallon plastic jerricans together [3/4 filled for flotation with tops well sealed] ready to be thrown into the water <u>on orders</u> having first been secured to the liferaft.

4. <u>ADDITIONAL EQUIPMENT</u> [which, other than an EPIRB, is normally in daily use]
    EPIRB; hand held VHF, Magellan GPS with spare battery pack
    binoculars; hand bearing compass, short wave radio with spare batteries
    Mini-C flashlight and Mini-C strobe light with spare batteries
    local and ocean charts in a waterproof case
    Sea Survival Manual; Raft Book; First Aid Manual; fish guidebook
    boat's papers and log; money, credit cards, passports

6. <u>LATEST FIX AND TRANSMIT DISTRESS CALLS</u> [normally the skipper's responsibility]

On abandoning ship wear long sleeved shirts, long trousers, and soft shoes. Depending on climate take insulating and shell layers, warm headdress or sunhats. Take personal medication if required, reading glasses if worn, sunglasses; watches; sailing knives; lifejackets. Restrict personal possessions to life preserving clothing and vital needs.

A CHILD OF WIND AND WATER

As my lists started to grow into a *Terrapin* compendium, I thought some wise thoughts on learning to sail a catamaran might be useful background reading for first time crew. Mercifully my homily never saw the light of day, but at that time it seemed a good idea. This was the start:

A cat is a boat. Just another boat. It behaves much as other boats behave, but a cat does have one fundamental difference compared to a keel boat. A cat is a child of wind and water. It floats <u>on</u> the water, not <u>in</u> the water. It responds, like a dancer in a disco, to every outside stimulus: wind, tide, and wave motion; and when the music stops, the cat will stop. It can lose way, abruptly; just as it can accelerate beyond the potential of a keel boat. At sea there is no heeling, there is no rolling, there is only an accommodation to the surface state of the ocean which can be good, and can, if you set your course on an unfortunate track, be hellish.

The absence of heel makes it difficult to realize the real force of the wind and real stress on the boat. So you must sail, in a sense, by numbers: you learn to reef when you hit something like 6 knots, or when the wind speed hits 15 knots: even if life is pleasant, the decks are dry, and you are still in your tee-shirt. Going into weather can be nightmarish. Waves at a certain frequency can set you 'hobby-horsing' wildly, and heading into steep seas can set up a millrace between the hulls with water slamming up against the bridgedeck, which is bad for you (for the noise is alarming), and not so good for the boat. The only answer is not to take it. Bear away. Find a better course.

And then I thought 'find a better course'? Why am I writing this? Just let people sail, that's the way you learn. None of us know anything at the start (and maybe we're still as foolish at the end) but sail. Get sailing.

Which leads me to my Commissioning Lists.

COMMISSIONING LISTS

NAVIGATION AND REFERENCE BOOKS

Chart No 1
Pilot Charts, ocean charts, approach charts, and harbor charts
Universal Plotting Sheets
Pilots and Coastal Pilots
weather guide
tide tables for cruising waters

star finder and Stellarscope
sextant
stopwatch; 2 x GMT watches
binoculars
hand bearing compass
Astrofix and spare batteries
2 x calculators and spare batteries

time, speed, and distance calculator
parallel rules, Douglas protractor; 2 x triangles
dividers; compasses; ruler
pens; pencils; pencil sharpener; erasers
magnifying glass
notebooks incl shorthand notebooks

log books
ship's papers in waterproof folder [with passports, emergency money etc]

NAVIGATION AND REFERENCE BOOKS

<u>On Board Reference Books</u>

manuals and handbooks for all equipment

Ocean Passages
World Cruising Routes
Ocean Crossing Guide
Reed's Nautical Almanac
Reed's Nautical Companion
US Coast Guard Navigation Rules
List of Radio Signals: Vol I Part I (Coast Radio Stations),
Part 2 (Radio Time Signals), and Vol 5

Sight Reduction Tables HO 249 (Vols 1, 2, and 3)
Petersen Guide to Astronomy
National Geographic star chart
Sun Sight Navigation, Arthur A Birney

Mariner's Guide to Single Sideband, Frederick Graves
BTI Maritime Handbook for Radio Operators
Icom SSB Guide
Marine VHF Operation, Michael Gale

Chapman Piloting
Chapman's Emergencies at Sea
The Boating Emergency Manual, Tony Meisel
The Yachtsman's Emergency Handbook, Neil Hallander
and Harold Mertes

NAVIGATION AND REFERENCE BOOKS

Rules of the Road, John Mellor
Quick Reference Nav Rules International and USA
Quick Reference Marine Electronics
Quick Reference Coastwise Piloting

Adlard Coles Heavy Weather Sailing
Handling Small Boats in Heavy Weather, Frank Robb

The 12V Bible, Miner Brotherton
The Care and Repair of Small Marine Diesels, Chris
Thompson

Advanced First Aid Afloat, Peter F Eastman, MD
First Aid for Yachtsmen, Dr Robert Haworth
The Pocket Doctor, Stephen Bezruchka, MD
DAN Underwater Diving Accident Manual
How to Cope with Dangerous Sea Life, Edwin S Iversen
and Renate Skinner

The Handbook of Sailing, Bob Bond
The Small Boat Skipper's Handbook, Geoff Lewis
The Boat Owner's Practical Dictionary, Denny Desoutter
Anchoring, Brian M Fagan

Baits, Rigs, and Tackle, Vic Dunaway
Fishes of the Atlantic Coast, Gar Goodson
Guide to Corals and Fishes of Florida, the Bahamas, and
the Caribbean, Idaz and Jerry Greenberg
Collectible Shells of Southeastern US, Bahamas, and the
Caribbean, R Tucker Abbott, PhD

NAVIGATION AND REFERENCE BOOKS

Guide to Flags of the World, Mauro Talocci
Courtesy Flags Made Easy, Mary Conger

All the relevant cruising guides and land guides as required
Yachtsman's Eight Language Dictionary

TOOL KIT AND SPARES

<u>main engines</u>
oil filters
fuel filters
alternator drive belts
gaskets and seals
injector
water pump impellers
hose clips
zincs
oil extractor pump
2 x engine cranking handles

<u>outboard</u>
shearpins and cotter pins
spark plugs
starting toggle

<u>electrical</u>
spare bulbs and repair kits for all nav lights, interior
lights, flashlights, and dive lights
spare fuses and circuit breakers
wiring kit
circuit tester
insulating tape
vinyl electrical tape
spare coil of wire of every gauge used on board

<u>repair kits</u>
gelcoat filler
GRP repair kit incl underwater epoxy and white and manilla gelcoat
fiberglass mats (different sizes)
Tinker Tramp repair kit
sailmaker's repair kit including needles and palm, sail cloth, sail thread, self-adhesive sail tape punch, grommets, and lead base for punch
scissors
wooden bungs (different sizes) for through-hull fittings
2 x spare bilge pump handles
crack cure adhesive
Super Epoxy
contact cement
PVC cement
marine sealant
rubbing compound
plastic polish
caulkstrip
chafing tape
duct tape
spare tape for making sail ties
adhesive tapes (white, red, green, yellow)
dummy Autohelm impeller [to plug log impeller through-hull fitting when servicing impeller

TOOL KIT AND SPARES

<u>rigging</u>
2 x spare winch handles
6 x spare mast-track slides
blocks, shackles, bottlescrews, bulldog clamps, and piston hanks [as spares]
split pins, cotter pins, clevis pins
roller reefing gear spares
jackstays and shackles
rigging cable and wire cutter

<u>cordage</u>
sheets and halliards
mooring lines
heaving line
whipping twine
nylon cord
rope gauge
ties
butane lighters
rigging tension gauge
nylon cord
nylon twine
nylon sail strips for making anchor rode markers
spare strapping
quoit for heaving line

<u>tools and maintenance</u>
main engine tool kit
outboard tool kit
full set of screwdrivers [straight cut and crosshead]
jewellers screwdrivers

Tool Kit and Spares

Allen keys
full set of spanners incl all small spanner sizes
socket wrench set [SAE and metric] with universal joint
full set of pliers incl flatnose and needlenose
vise grips: large and needlenose
adjustable crescent wrenches (10, 8, and 6 in)
hammer
short handled sledge hammer
hand drill with full set of bits
hack saw and spare blades incl wood blades
files: round and flat 6 in
trimming knife and spare blades
Stanley knife and spare blades
universal deck key
centre punch
awl (or ice pick)
wire cutters
nicopress tool with sleeves
soldering iron with solder
upholstery needle
galvanized wire
copper wire
self-tapping screws [all sizes]
wood screws [all sizes]
bolts [all sizes]
locking washers and nuts [all sizes]
tape measure
paint brushes
sandpapers
wet and dry
wood filler

hose clips [all sizes on board]
plastic tubing [odd lengths and sizes as might be required]
spare lengths of engine tubing particularly cooling circuit hoses
spare copper tubing and flexible gas pipe tubing with clips and sealant
2 x spare hurricane lamp glasses and spare wicks
plastic ties [all sizes]
shock cord and bungies

miscellaneous
auxiliary steering arm
Ampair water turbine mounting ring
spare conversion mounting bolts and nuts for Ampair
spare Ampair water turbine
plastic covered cables with nico-pressed eyes and marine padlocks for securing inflatable [and outboard to inflatable] when on shore
scuba gear spares
fishing rod, reel, and line spares with maintenance kit

fuel, lubricants and distilled water
diesel
main engine oil
main engine transfer case oil
gas for outboard
outboard oil mix
Yamaha gearbox oil (SAE 90)
propane
hurricane and oil lamp fuel

TOOL KIT AND SPARES

marine grease
silicone grease and pasta
WD40
656 lubricant
Teflon lubricant
electrical grade lubricant
LPS grades 1, 2, and 3
penetrating oil
cleaning fluid (lighter fluid or white spirit)
degreaser
distilled water
plastic tool box
fishing tackle box for odd shackles, nuts, bolts, screws
and minor fixings

<u>spare dry cell batteries</u> [the only way is to list everything
that needs batteries, rather like this]

<u>AAA</u>

Pelican lights (x2)	(4)	AAA total 6
magnifying glass	(2)	

<u>AA</u>

Astrofix pack	(4)	AA total 27
Magellan	(6)	alkaline +
alarm clock	(1)	*non-alkaline 2
Astra IIIB	(2)*	
battery razor	(2)	
Sony ICF-SW1S	(6)	
CD player	(2)	
Sunpak dive flash	(6)	

<u>C</u>

Mini-C (x2)	(8)	C	total	16
Pelican 2-cell halogen	(2)			
Mini-C strobe	(2)			
CD aux speakers	(4)			

<u>D</u>

Sony radio cassette	(6)	D	total	10
PFD lights (x4)	(4)			

<u>6V Rayovac No 945</u>

Danbuoy strobe	(1)	9V	total	1

<u>miscellaneous batteries</u>

Astrofix	2 x lithium CR-2032
Casio nav watch	SR927W
Casio dive watch	lithium CR2320
stopwatch	UCC392/SR41W
Firefly rescue light	ACR Mercury E&B 10410
Casio Data-Cal	CR2025
Tasco binoculars	Eveready 389/SR54
Nikonos-V	1 x 3V lithium CR 1/3N type or 2 x 1.55V silver-oxide SR-44 or 2 x 1.5V alkaline-manganese LR 44
Olympus Infinity	6V Panasonic lithium CR-P2

MEDICAL [*prescription drugs]

PAIN KILLERS
*Tylox	for severe pain
*APAP and Codeine	for moderate pain
Adult Analgesic (Anacin)	for headaches, slight pain

TRANQUILIZER
*Lorazepam	calmative, similar to Valium, will make you sleepy

INFECTION
*Dicloxacillin	antibiotic to control wound infection: coral cuts and wounds that won't heal
*Amoxicillin	antibiotic to control any respiratory infection

STOMACH COMPLAINTS
Immodium	for diarrhea
*Donnatal	for generalized stomach cramps or nausea (smooth muscle relaxant)
*Doxycycline	for prolonged diarrhea or urinary tract infection (antibiotic)
Senokot	laxative, to relieve constipation
Maalox	to relieve indigestion
Dioralyte	to restore electrolyte balance after diarrhea

BURNS

*Silvadene cream	for severe sunburn or generalized burns, to be used under sterile dressing if necessary
Mediquik	spray anesthetic for minor burns or bruising when skin is unbroken

EYES

AK Rinse	sterile eye wash, squirt straight from bottle
*Erythromycin Opthal ointment	for eye infection
*Ak-taine drops	unaesthetic for eyes or more general use: <u>must be kept cool after use</u>

EARS

*Octicair Otic Suspension	for swimmer's ear or any ear ache

JELLYFISH OR INSECT STINGS

*EpiPen	Epinephrine Auto-Injector for anaphylaxis [allergic emergencies]. [use in preference to Anaphylaxis Emergency Treatment Kit]

*Anaphylaxis Emergency
Treatment Kit
for anaphylaxic shock
[severe cases of reaction to
insect bite or jellyfish sting]
[follow instructions]

Sea Sting
Sting Kill
Meat Tenderizer
apply neat to stung area:
can give allergy tablets in
conjunction if patient
distressed or showing signs
of obvious swelling

ANTIHISTAMINE
Allergy tablets
for hay fever; and reaction
to jellyfish stings or insect
bites

ANTIBIOTIC CREAM
Bacitracin
for small wounds with any
infection

ANTISEPTICS
Povidine-Iodine Solution
same as Betadine. dilute
1:4 solution: boiled water.
use to cleanse around
wound. can be used neat,
but do not get any in wound
itself as it stings horribly.

Antiseptic wipes
for cleaning small wounds
before applying ointment
or Band Aid

Dettol cream	for minor scratches and cuts
Alcohol wipes	always use before giving injections, or general area cleansing
Medicated soap	use to wash hands carefully before beginning any dressings or surgical procedure

DRESSINGS

Multi trauma dressings	for massive open wound
Army field dressings	for staunching bleeding quickly
Sterile dressings	various sizes depending on size of wound, to be bandaged on top
Eye pads	
Surgical gauze pads	
Adhesive pads	
Band Aids	waterproof, various sizes and shapes
Steristrips	to draw skin surfaces together on sides of cut or wound

BANDAGES

Ace bandages	2 in and 4 in
Stretch gauze and Kling	
Triangular	
Crepe	
Gauze	

DENTAL FIRST AID
all purpose pack   follow instructions given

SEA SICKNESS
*Transderm Scop   patches for placement
                                    behind ear

Triptone
Stugeron
Ginger 500mg   health food capsules.
                                    take 2 every 3 hours

COUGHS AND COLDS
Cold capsules   equivalent to Contac. can
                                    make you drowsy

Sore throat lozenges
Sudafed   decongestant

SUNBURN
Zinc oxide cream
*Silvadene
Solarcaine

INSECT REPELLENTS
Jungle Formula   liquid and gel

VITAMINS
Thera-Plus   multi vitamins. 1 daily

MISCELLANEOUS
Scissors

Tweezers — chisel ended and sharp ended

Thermometer

Prethreaded surgical needles — for sutures

Disposable syringes and needles

Two spare needles — for removing small splinters

Scalpel blades

Surgical gloves — to be used when sterile conditions are necessary

Safety pins

Sam splint — can be formed to shape of appropriate limb, then bandage to hold firmly, not tightly

Finger splint — bandage lightly to hold in place

Cotton wool

Q-tips

Magnifying glass

Scotch tape for humans — use to hold dressings in place

Vaseline

Pocket mask — for mouth to mouth or oxygen to mouth resuscitation

Book matches

Eye glass repair kit

Medicated powder — good for prickly heat

Handcream

Glucose tablets

Salt tablets

Sun screens — <u>note creams or lotions only</u> (gels and oils affect fiberglass)

EMERGENCY SURVIVAL PACKS

emergency First Aid kit [incl Solarcaine and sea sickness pills]
high protection sun cream
survival rations, hard tack biscuits
glucose tablets, multi-vitamin tablets, vitamin C tablets
concentrated lemon
beef extract
plastic sheeting for rain collection, funnel, and collapsible containers for water
duct tape
flares and smoke signals, dye markers, whistle
Firefly Rescue Light or strobe light and spare batteries
small compass on lanyard
Pelican light and spare batteries
mirror for signalling
nylon cord
waterproof matches and butane lighter
knife, scissors
small chopping board
plastic containers with lids
zip-lock bags
enamel or metal bowls (2)
plastic mugs (4)
one pint screw top jar (as in-use water bottle)
table knives, forks, and spoons (2 of each)
can openers (2)
crown bottle opener

all-purpose survival tool
whipping twine
space blankets (2)
spare sunglasses
salt water soap
Sea Survival manual

survival pack fishing tackle [the list shows exactly what I keep packed in my survival box]
150ft 340 lb test handline and 1 monofilament handline with weight and 3 hooks
100yds 100 lb test monofilament line
100m 22 kg test monofilament line
3 x 24in 60 lb test leaders
6 x No 4 hooks with wire leaders
set of 3 mackerel hooks (different sizes) + leader
3 x Dolphin trolling lures (2 with leaders) + 1 sardine lure
2 x jigger hooks
4 x spare weights
fish stringer, fish scaler, fishing pliers, multi-purpose fishing tool
small gaff and small fish billy

survival water
hand operated watermaker, or
minimum of 4 x 2 gal water cans [3/4 filled for flotation with tops well sealed] lashed together on a line for attachment to liferaft

HOUSEKEEPING

nonstick cooking pans incl frying pan, medium and small saucepan, all with vented lids, small saucepan, small iron skillet, whistling kettle, coffee pot, baking tray, and pressure cooker
plastic crockery, coffee mugs, plastic glasses, insulated plastic glasses, insulated can holders
individual cereal/salad/desert bowls

knives, forks, spoons [incl 2 sets for survival pack] and chopsticks
kitchen knives, wooden spoons, ladle, egg beater, grater, bottle opener, can openers [incl 2 can openers for survival pack], twist opener, corkscrew, ice pick, orange squeezer, grapefruit knife

sieve, steamer
set of 2 nesting mixing/serving bowls, salad bowl
food and drink containers [incl set for survival pack], fruit juice container
measuring jug
3 chopping boards [incl 1 small for survival pack]
kitchen timer
wide mouthed and normal size unbreakable Thermos jars

garbage bags, zip-lock bags, polyethylene bags, paper towels [vast supply of paper towels!]
garbage pail
washing up brush, scourers, J cloths, rubber gloves
drying up cloths
oven gloves or pot holders
waterproof matches, stove lighter, butane lighters [incl matches & 1 lighter for survival pack]

222

Lemon Joy (can be used in salt water), Fantastic, Windex, Pledge

cleaning liquids, Swarfega or equivalent for taking oil and grease off skin

dust pan and brush, small wet/dry vacuum cleaner

scrubbing brush, sponges, rags

deck swab or squeegee,

bucket with lanyard

biodegradable toilet paper, toilet brush, toilet plunger

white vinegar for cleaning toilet bowl (it will not affect plumbing and pipes)

holding tank biodegradable active agent

boat cleaning materials including green scouring pads

washing machine detergent, cold water washing powder, travel wash

clothes pegs and clothes line, clothes hangers

iron and sewing kit

sleeping bags (zip-together?)

fitted sheets

sheet blankets

pillows, pillow cases

towels

soap, salt water soap, shampoo

hair dryer

mosquito coils, bug spray

lightweight backpack(s) for shopping

SPECIFICATION OF *TERRAPIN*

Heavenly Twins 27. Special Edition. Capability:
World-Wide cruising.

OUTLINE SPECIFICATION

LOA 27 ft.0. LWL 21 ft 6in. Beam 13 ft 9in. Draft unladen 2 ft 3in. Draft fully laden 2 ft 7 ins. Unladen weight 2.5 tons. Masthead height 36 ft 0in. GPS antenna height (topmost point on boat) 37 ft ASL. Sails: genoa area 260 sq ft; staysail/storm jib 32 sq ft; mainsail area 130 sq ft; cruising chute 550 sq ft. Centre cockpit. Headroom 6 ft 3in in hulls; 5 ft 8in in saloon entrance. Two separate aft cabins or aft stateroom for 2. Other berths: 2. Twin Yanmar 1GM10 diesels.

DOCUMENTATION

US registration documented in Miami, Florida. US Documentation Number: 960675. Hull Identification Number: HT 2704550390. Sail Number: 455. Callsign: WAJ 9493. Home Port: Tequesta, Florida.

DETAILED SPECIFICATION

Hand moulded GRP hull & deck with hull in Scott Bader Super White 337 with a cove line Scott Bader Super Black 630 and non-slip deck panels in Scott Bader Manilla 3952. Hull and deck one piece mouldings with CSM/Woven Rovings sandwich for strength and lightness with top quality isopthalic resins, join bonded with 6oz CSM creating an immensely strong monocoque structure with sealed buoyancy chambers forward and aft, and in the leading half of each keel. All forward buoyancy chambers foam filled. Extra layup to keels and skegs, and keels additionally reinforced at the forefoot. Keel shoes fitted to each keel (sacrificial hardwood timber bearers on keel bottoms, glassed over). Antifouling Scott Bader - Ferro Corp Copperclad (environmentally clean copper impregnated hull coating which has extra resistance to water penetration and osmosis and lasts at least 15 years). Bridge deck, fore and side decks, and coachroofs end grain balsa GRP sandwich for strength, stiffness, and insulation. Substantial plywood pads bonded into deck fitting positions. GRP moulded cockpit weather shielding with opening plexiglass windows and attachment for bimini. Lifting out strop positions marked on hulls fore and aft.

Aluminum and hard rubber rubbing strakes, teak grabrails, four 10 1/2in and two 8in alloy deckcleats, with seven alloy fairleads, large double bow roller with retaining pin, and a manual anchor winch. Four solar ventilators. Two large self-draining foredeck lockers (for ground tackle and 2 x 10lb propane tanks). Cleats for all lines led to the cockpit. Three large cockpit lockers. Four cockpit drains. All through-hull drains protected against surge through slamming by deflector shielding. Helmsman's seat. U bolt for safety harness in cockpit. Semi-permanent jacklines on side decks. Harness for Tinker Tramp inflatable on foredeck. 24in stainless steel pulpits and stern rails (one with a flagpole socket), and stanchions with double lifelines and Pelican hook releases at the cockpit and at the transom. Horseshoe lifebuoy with whistle and ocean dye marker on lifelines by helmsman connected to Danbuoy and self-activating strobe light. Stainless steel hinged boarding ladder fitted at the transom. Stainless steel grabrail over saloon doors. 25 lb CQR with 50ft chain and 175ft nylon anchor rode. 11 kg Studland with 20ft chain and 145ft nylon rode. Six large fenders. Two 25 ft and two 50 ft 1/2in nylon warps.

Alloy mast (29 ft 6 in) mounted in hinged step, with two halyard winches, spinnaker crane fitting, and internal wiring conduit, radar reflector, lightning protection, and mast steps. Stainless steel boom gallows with cruising chute blocks at base. Masthead tri-color sailing, steaming, and anchor lights, spreader lights, and cockpit light. VHF and GPS antennas. Stainless steel chainplates and standing rigging, double backstays (one insulated for SSB antenna), cap and lower shrouds, inner and outer forestay, with toggles, rigging screws, and plastic shroud rollers. All normal running rigging including mainsheet purchase with jam cleat and full width track and slider, slider control lines and cleats, topping lift, genoa sheet tracks, fairleads, cleats, sliders, and turning blocks. Lewmar 16 self-tailing winch with locking handle and handle pocket. 260 sq ft genoa fitted to a high quality roller reefing gear, with furling lines, blocks, and cleats. Roller reefing 32 sq ft staysail/storm jib with track, slider, and all controls and lines. 130 sq ft mainsail with two rows of slab reefing with Lazy Jacks. 550 sq ft cruising chute. Bimini, with extra zip-on side curtains, designed to serve additionally as a rainwater catchment, secured to cockpit hardtop and lashed to boom gallows at trailing edge.

Autohelm ST-50 sailing instruments: speed/log module, depth module, wind module, and steering compass module in cockpit. Magnetic steering compass in cockpit. Vetus stainless steel wheel with heavy duty rack and pinion steering system, stainless steel internal tie bar, and standby steering system. Autohelm 4000 autopilot with remote. Twin Yanmar 1GM10 9 hp diesels with 12V 10kW Hitachi starter motors and 35A alternators mounted in each hull under the cockpit driving twin 2-bladed 13 in x 9 in propellers fitted with strippers (cutting blades) on the shafts. Two entirely separate dedicated 55AHC engine starting batteries. Two Yanmar Type A instrument panels supplemented with separate VDO tachometers with built-in hour meters. Two 16 gallon fuel tanks giving an endurance of approximately 180 hours per tank. Lighting, automatic BCF fire extinguishers, and deckhead eyes and lifting tackle for maintenance in each engine compartment.

Through-bolted tinted Lexan windows in saloon and aft cabins with additional Lewmar opening portlights in the galley, heads, nav area, saloon deckhead, and aft cabins. Two tinted plexiglass windows in saloon doors. Toughened tinted acrylic hatch over saloon table. All interior woodwork light ash with solid teak trim. 4in foam filled cushions in saloon and in aft cabins finished in Sahara (light beige) hard wearing water resistant material. Carpeted throughout below decks. Saloon seats and table convertable to a double berth if required, or two single berths. Built-in bar stowage forward of saloon table, and a built-in cassette rack in the saloon. Navigation area with fold-down nav table, side lockers, book and pencil shelves, and chart stowage. Halon fire extinguisher in nav area. Twin aft double cabins with 3.5ft x 7ft berths convertable to one single aft stateroom with a 7ft x 7ft bed. Fitted sheets for all berths. Generous locker space.

Icom M56 VHF radio. Icom M700 SSB radio. Magellan GPS Nav 5000 with alternative positions in nav area and cockpit. Autohelm ST-50 Multi-Function display in nav area. Lokata Watchman radar alarm. 30A 110/125V 60 Hz stainless steel shore power inlet with 50 ft shore power cord. 30A AC circuit breaker and polarity warning indicator. Battery charger and isolator. 110/125V outlets with GFI in the galley, saloon, nav area, and aft cabins. 250W frequency controlled inverter. Multi-battery condition meter. DC input and output ammeters. 12V circuit breaker panel and illuminated switch panel. Two Swiftec ground plates. Four 12v 1.2A 6 in oscillating fans (in galley, nav area, and aft cabins). 12V outlets in the galley, saloon, cockpit, and aft cabins. Full internal lights with additional red lights in nav area and galley for night passage making. Ampair Aquair 100 wind/water turbine generator, stern mounted, with an additional eye and stern rail fitment for water turbine use. Two Solarex MSX-Lite 18 solar panels with solar monitor and regulator. All wiring accessible through conduits. 2 x 85 AHC house batteries. AFI electronic weather station. Regatta barometer, hygrometer, and clock.

Fully fitted galley with propane double burner stove with broiler and oven, twin sinks, hot and cold fresh water, sea water wash, plate and glass racks, Formica work surfaces, and all normal storage. Extra large 12V

Supercool box. Halon fire extinguisher and fire blanket in galley. Two 36 gallon aluminum water tanks (with 8 additional 2-gallon water cans). Propane on-demand water heater in galley. Gas detector and alarm. Fully fitted heads with hand sink and shower with hot and cold pressurized fresh water, and electric shower sump pump. Electric sea toilet discharging through a macerator pump and Y-valve either to a 10 gallon holding tank or directly outboard (holding tank can be pumped out at dockside or discharged at sea). Manual option to toilet. Two manual and two electric bilge pumps.

Fully fitted sailing/rowing version of Tinker Tramp with additional liferaft conversion: inflatable high visibility survival canopy, CO_2 inflation, and SOLAS sea anchor. Yamaha 4hp outboard fitted on bracket on transom. Dive tank racks for four 80 cuft dive tanks fitted in the cockpit.

DESIGN AND BUILD
Heavenly Twins designed by Pat Patterson. *Terrapin* moulded by Armada Plastics, Plymouth, Devon, England, built by Martyn Medcalf, Cornish Catamarans, Redruth, Cornwall, and launched 8 March 1990. Refits and modifications carried out by Virgin Gorda Yacht Services, Virgin Gorda, BVI, and Stuart Yacht Builders Inc, Stuart, Florida. Cruising fit design Mathew Wilson.